The Fantastical Engineer

The Fantastical Engineer

Engineer

A Thrillseeker's Guide to Careers in Theme Park Engineering

Celeste Baine

Professional Publications, Inc. • Belmont, CA

THE FANTASTICAL ENGINEER
A THRILLSEEKER'S GUIDE TO CAREERS
IN THEME PARK ENGINEERING

Current printing of this edition: 4

Printing History

edition number	printing number	update
1	2	Reprinted.
1	3	Reprinted.
1	4	Minor corrections. Copyright update.

Printed in the United States of America

Professional Publications, Inc.
1250 Fifth Avenue, Belmont, CA 94002
(650) 593-9119
www.ppi2pass.com

ISBN: 1-59126-021-3

CIP Pending

Other Career Books by Professional Publications, Inc.

Engineering Your Writing Success
How Engineers Can Master Effective On-the-Job
Communication Skills

Engineering Your Start-Up
A Guide for the High-Tech Entrepreneur

Is There an Engineer Inside You?
A Comprehensive Guide to Career Decisions in Engineering

Is There a Materials Engineer Inside You?
A Student's Guide to Exploring Materials Engineering

Is There a Mechanical Engineer Inside You?
A Student's Guide to Exploring Mechanical Engineering

Is There a Chemical Engineer Inside You?
A Student's Guide to Exploring Chemical Engineering

Is There a Biomedical Engineer Inside You?
A Student's Guide to Exploring Biomedical Engineering

Is There an Electrical Engineer Inside You?
A Student's Guide to Exploring Electrical Engineering

Is There a Civil Engineer Inside You?
A Student's Guide to Exploring Civil Engineering

To order from Professional Publications, Inc.:

www.ppi2pass.com
1-800-426-1178

Dedication

To all the Lincoln
Berry's of this world.

Acknowledgments

I would like to extend my thanks to the many entertainment companies that helped make this book a reality. I can't list every person that made my research possible the list is too long. However, I would like to extend my special thanks to Lincoln Berry III, Nathan Naversen of ITEC Productions, Peter iNova of Metavision, Richard Graham of Projex International, Dave Graul of Attraction Services, Ken Lucci of Lucci & Associates, Beth Shery of the American Institute of Chemical Engineers, Stewart Zillerberg of Scenery West, Maris Ensing of Mad Systems, Chris Gray of CMG Models, Will Pedersen of Rando Productions, Paul Mulder of Illusion Engineering, Courtney Millburn of International Aquatic Consultants, Peter McDonnell of Tilden Lobnitz Cooper, Mark Hanlon of Hanlon Engineering, Frank Weigand of Frank Weigand & Associates, Bob Chambers of It's Alive Co., and EA & Bullfrog.

This book was made possible by the enthusiasm of the entertainment industry and constant support I received to jump the next hurdle. I also want to thank Linda Ramsey for giving me almost unlimited flexibility in scheduling.

I want to thank my Mom and Dad, Carol Lum, MaryAnn Bratschi, Amy Siddon, and all my friends that provided the support, insight, and encouragement to keep writing.

Acknowledgments of Lincoln Berry III

I have long desired to combine my knowledge of Video Game Design with conventional ride technology to create a fully-immersive experience and a totally new breed of amusement attraction. Over ten years ago, my good friend Ben Anderson and I would dream of the roller coasters that will populate the theme parks of the next century.

Today I would like to extend a heartfelt thanks to all my family, especially Mom and Dad. And to my brother Tad for his selfless technical support.

My special thanks to the Avery family, Robert Senior and his beloved wife, Rob "Loonitic" Avery, the up-and-coming king of all horror films and dedicated friend who helped me conquer many a roller coaster, and to "Princess" Aleta, for her spiritual support.

An extended thanks to Danielle Godale for believing, and to William and Carmen Buckman for guidance.

And to my Internet pal, the ingenious Kevin Teufer for his correspondence from Florida, his expertise with the amusement industry, and for his brilliant insight.

Thanks to Jim Oliver for hosting my essay at Commkey Network and huge thanks to Celeste Baine and Bonamy Publishing for giving me this opportunity and publishing my essay.

Roller Coaster pictures by Chris Gray.

About This Book

This book is a source of compiled information to help you search for glamour jobs in engineering. There is currently no book like it. It is about applying a foundation of engineering knowledge and study, adding a creative spin, and landing a dream job.

Although mostly about theme park engineering, this book also touches on entertainment engineering in general. You will find the majority of pages relate to theme parks, but entertainment can also include aquariums, zoos, casinos, sporting events, trade shows, museums, cinemas and restaurants such as the Hard Rock Cafe and Planet Hollywood. The majority of employers listed do not limit themselves to theme park design. They encompass a wide range of creative activities such as scenery fabrication, mechanical systems, special effects, fiber-optic lighting design, audio/video design, show control systems, manufacturing, software programming, and pyrotechnics just to name a few.

The opportunities available for engineers in this industry are as varied as there are engineers. Positions are available for many different types of engineers including computer engineers, industrial engineers, ride and show engineers, project engineers, architectural engineers, electrical engineers, software engineers, mechanical engineers, structural engineers, and audio/video engineers. Engineers are needed to design the face of what the public sees as well as to support the business of theme parks such as crowd control, research and development, training, and equipment maintenance.

This is a resource book. On many pages you will find descriptions of some of the companies that hire engineers in the entertainment field. I advise reading through these descriptions to get an overall feel for the industry and to see what sparks your interest. These companies and their contact information are listed in the appendix. The listings are current as of January 2000. Every entertainment based company that hires engineers could not possibly be listed, but there are enough to jump-start your search as you learn more about the industry and develop networking contacts.

CONTENTS

Introduction

Thrillrides for the 21st Century

by Lincoln Berry III

Imagine yourself harnessing into an inverted steel-looping coaster. Attached to the headrest is a Virtual Reality Head Mounted Display (HMD) that lowers over your head just as the harness does. Also mounted to the seat beside you is a joystick, mocked-up to look like an F-16 flight stick. You drop the HMD over your head, and suddenly you are immersed in a "Star Wars" themed virtual universe (you can choose not to wear the HMD if you prefer the natural terrain!)

The robust theme song of Star Wars pulses in your ears with the familiar chant of royal brass. As the coaster climbs the hill, you are briefed on your mission: To attack the dreaded Death Star and disable the ominous weapon of destruction. The words scroll under you like a monolith and dissolve into the vastness of space. In your personal, virtual world, you are an X-Wing fighter pilot. You take hold of the joystick and grip firmly.

You reach the top of the hill, and then – DROP! As you make your 170-foot descent, inside your virtual world, you experience the famous "trench battle" scene all around you! You drop into the trench of the mighty death star – Tie fighter engines screaming like banshees all around you! Laser blasts pounding, lighting up the space around you like the fourth of July! Subwoofers attached to the seat pulsate with each blast, sending thunder through your bones!

You enter the second 90-foot vertical loop, and you see Darth Vader approaching you fast! Squeeze the trigger and blast his minions to smithereens. Vader is on your tail as you go into a cobra roll – his turbo lasers threatening to send you into oblivion!

Into the corkscrew and helix, you fight the joystick as your X-Wing buckles from the G-Forces. Watch it! You narrowly missed that trench wall! A half-second too late, and you would have been flatter than if Jaba the Hut had sat on you.

Coming out of the final heartline roll, you see your target – The reactor vent itself. You are moving so fast. The voice of your sensei Ben Kenobi whispers in your ear, "Use the Force!" But do you have the skill to knock the target out? Suddenly the ride is over, the coaster pulls into the loading station and the scores are tallied. Who will be king among the Jedi's today?

Engineering

Entertainment

Chapter One

Theme Park Design 101

If you have ever visited a theme park on the opening day of a new attraction, I'm sure you remember

the anticipation as you waited for your turn. The screaming, giggling and anxious 11 year-olds next to you are unable to contain their excitement. The look of exhilaration and the sound of laughter of the people who just finished the ride before you add to your suspense. You have been waiting all day to feel the deafening beat of your own heart and the anticipation of strapping yourself into the bucket and letting the ride begin. Your whole body awakens and your spirit soars to learn and explore a secret part of itself. This thrill is beyond expectation, orchestrated in a perfectly and completely safe environment.

That kind of special connection with your guests is a result of touching their emotions. The real magic of pulling off such an event is in the storytelling. Technology can make us ooh and ahh but can not be compared with a compelling story. As an e-factor or entertainment engineer, you must move your audience to tears, laughter, excitement, fear, or exhilaration. It is an amazing and unique blend of art and science by people who are passionate about bringing their's and other's ideas to life. Peter iNova and Nathan Naversen will show you how to create a compelling story and touch the emotions of your audience in chapters two and three.

The great arm of engineering can reach out to us all in every imaginable way. Engineering surrounds

---

Offering a wide range of solutions in the fields of animation & ride control, audio and video systems, motion simulator technology and systems integration, Anitech's approach to hardware design and system architecture stresses both reliability and ease of maintenance to achieve unsurpassed "uptime" and maintainability. Anitech's flagship product, the MediaPro 4000, sets a new standard for digital animation, audio, lighting and show control for the themed entertainment industry.

-Anitech Systems, Inc.

and astounds us. It constantly challenges what we have achieved and dares us to take the next step forward into the unknown. E-factor engineering can be compared to making the square peg fit into the round hole. Often, in themed environments, corners are not square, structures may be intentionally crooked, and the traditional straightedge must be scrapped.

Many professionals pursue e-factor engineering because of the glamour, gizmos, or sex appeal. In this case, sex appeal does not mean X-rated. Sex appeal refers to the glamour and Hollywood feel of the industry. Entertainment is designed to make people feel inspired, dazzled, wondrous, loved, and above all, to feel-the-rush. Many engineers pursue it because they are interested in how things work, taking things apart or solving problems. Many love going to theme parks, amusement parks, science centers, aquariums, zoos, etc. Many love seeing the latest high-tech movies or are fascinated by lights and special effects. Whatever your reason may be for liking it, there is a place for you

Design of heating, ventilation, air conditioning, plumbing, water effects, fire protection systems and support for special effects systems. Design through construction documents for recording studios, sound stages, exhibit spaces, retail and restaurant spaces, amusement attractions, indoor rides, theaters, etc. Consultation, concept, design developement as well as "Design-Build" packages available for above.
-M B & A Consulting Mechanical Engineers

in this field. However, nobody said it was going to be easy. We'll talk more about your future as an e-factor engineer and how to break into this industry in chapter four.

The excitement of opening your attraction to the public as well as exploiting the technologies of the future make e-factor engineering a dream job. In the spirit of creativity, you work hard, innovate, and bring imagination to life for millions of friends and families in the world. Your job of making people happy can be highly contagious as one smile usually leads to another. According to Bob Thomas, author of *Walt Disney, An American Original*, "Walt rejected a design for one building with the comment: 'I think the fellow was attempting to monument himself rather than designing something that is for people.' Walt impressed on his designers again and again that he wasn't seeking architectural masterpieces. 'All I want you to think about,' he told them, 'is that when people walk through or ride through or have access to anything you design, I want

Harmonix Music Systems, Inc., a Cambridge-based company with roots at MIT's Media Lab, is shattering the boundaries of interactive music through its revolutionary music-making technology. Harmonix is working with the world's leading entertainment and technology companies to develop interactive music applications for arcades, theme parks, game consoles and PC's.

-Harmonix Music Systems, Inc.

them, when they leave, to have smiles on their faces. Just remember that; it's all I ask of you as a designer.'"

In this industry you need to get ready to work hard and put in long hours. Project based entertainment fabrication is full of deadlines and details. According to Maris Ensing of Mad Systems, the most important skill an engineering student can acquire is "no need for sleep, if that can be cultivated as a skill."

Entertainment companies are upsizing and downsizing or hiring consultants because their needs change every time a new attraction is contracted. The market is very competitive. "You need all the skills you can get. Straight electrical, electronics, computer skills, software, mechanical, optical, anything you can learn: do it! Learn to learn. It's up to you to make it happen, and it's up to you to make sure they happen right. Almost right is not an option. From incoming wiring to speaker wiring to amplifiers, lighting, dimmers, strobes, special effects, sensors, grounding, emergency stops,

Leisure and Recreation Concepts, Inc. (LARC) specializes in the research, planning, design/architectural, construction coordination and management of amusement and entertainment projects including theme parks, water parks, family entertainment centers, shopping mall attractions, and aquariums. Services include economic feasibility studies, master plans, renderings, construction budgets, consulting, management, staffing, training and equipment procurement.

-Leisure & Recreation Concepts/LARC, Inc.

computers, motion bases, projectors, smoke machines, hanging, fixing and mounting things to whatever crazy thing you bump into next. Do it as well as you can, and make sure it's as good as it needs to be! By the time the job is in and you leave the site, be proud of the part you've played in it," said Ensing.

The attraction must perfectly mimic a faraway world not only on opening day but also for many years to come. Fortunately, the process of creating, inventing, and spinning attractions can be so much fun that maybe you won't notice you are actually working. For example, the conceptual designer might say to you, "I want the guests to smell bananas on King Kong's breath." As an engineer, you will work from that point and determine the feasibility of an effect from the perspective of safety, reliability, guest impact, and budget. Most likely you won't need to wear a tie or skirt everyday, and the constant challenge will keep you from falling into a humdrum routine.

Another effective way to set out to entertain millions in the future is by putting your story down on paper, any paper. Use your scratch pad, notebook, the

---

Degreed engineer with 30 years of machine design & management experience. Includes over ten years in conceptual design, technical management, design audits, installation supervision, and field upgrades of complex shows, rides and animation.

-Frank Weigand & Associates

wallpaper, napkins, anything. Just get it down and let the process of engineering begin. Open your mind and sketch from your heart. Explore, experiment, and extend yourself, but don't be afraid to create or to make mistakes. According to Marty Sklar, Vice Chairman of Imagineering for Walt Disney, "Everyone starts with a blank piece of paper. There are two ways to look at a blank sheet of paper. You can look at it as the most frightening thing in the world, or as the greatest opportunity in the world because nobody's put anything on it."

Get in practice creating things from your imagination. If you can draw it, make a model, or build a prototype, then you can build the real thing. The important concept is to get in the habit of making your ideas tangible. This book is about engineering the fantastical. The only limits are ones you impose upon yourself. You must dare to dream and be prepared to run with your ideas.

TLC is a multi-discipline engineering firm providing aquatic, mechanical, electrical, plumbing, and structural engineering design services for waterparks, theme parks, attractions, rides, retail shops and resort hotels. Our goal is to provide innovative, cost effective systems solutions that meet operational and project team requirements. TLC offers design services throughout the U.S. and abroad.

-Tilden Lobnitz Cooper

Richard Graham, president of Projex International advises, "Stop and look at what already exists, what works and what doesn't. A day at the local theme park is a day at the office. Typically the best engineering in a park is the hardest to find. It sometimes helps to snoop around behind the scenes. Don't break the law, but usually mornings are best to look at equipment that is being maintained, repaired, or upgraded."

Feature Article - Engineering Today's and Tomorrow's Entertainment

by Beth Shery

Fabulous Film Effects

Computer engineers and animators are creating effects that can amuse and amaze even the most jaded audiences. Jurassic Park in 1993, Forrest Gump and Interview with the Vampire in 1994. Advanced computer graphics imagery (CGI) has moved far beyond what audiences could imagine just a few

Rando Productions, Inc. is a full service company incorporating all elements relating to mechanical systems design and engineering, hydraulic engineering, and scenic fabrication with an emphasis on large show action equipment fabrication for the theme park and film industries.

-Rando Productions, Inc.

years ago. The field has grown enormously since Disney's TRON, which was set inside a video game, first explored the technique in 1982. The CGI dinosaurs in Jurassic Park were engineered to be photo-realistic in every detail, from muscles moving when they breathed, to their eyes looking wet.

But, the CGI technique most talked about is "morphing," which debuted in Willow in 1988, transforming a tiger into a woman. Other examples include an Exxon ad in which a car changes into a running tiger, face melding in Godley & Creme's Cry, the first music video to use morphing, and the shape-shifting liquid-metal cyborg in Terminator 2.

Many scenes in Forrest Gump used morphing technology. For example, the character of Lieutenant Dan, after losing the lower portion of both legs, is seen being lifted out of bed and dangling off the side of a shrimp boat. While the actor has full use of his legs, his stumps and the side of the boat (there was a section cut in the boat so he could swing his real legs through. Then, the boat was electronically "filled-in") were digitally mastered to appear realistic.

Gump interacts with many historical figures, including Presidents

Kennedy and Johnson. Special effects artists matched the grainy textures of archival film footage and morphed the lip movements of the presidents to match the new words being spoken by actors.

More and more television commercials are also using elaborate CGI, such as the polar bears in Coca-Cola ads, the Listerine bottle swinging through the air on a vine, and the Pillsbury Doughboy.

Hollywood Meets Silicon Valley

Interactive television-the ability to pick and choose whatever programs, films, or games you want from over 500 channels-is coming to a TV near you. Features will include interactive news and educational programs, along with the ability to access videos on demand. And, interactive feature films will allow audiences to choose a film's outcome. Engineers are involved in all aspects of this technology, from designing new cables to creating new film emulsions to engineering better sound quality.

Multimedia design and production for web sites, theme parks, museums, and point-of-purchase applications.

-Harvest Moon Studio

*Beth G. Shery of the American Institute
of Chemical Engineers.*

Engineering is one of the most progressive, challenging, and rewarding fields that can be studied today. Engineers work to improve the quality of life or to make life more efficient, comfortable, or fun. They strive for constant improvement by applying scientific principles such as physics, electronics, thermodynamics, fluids, or heat transfer to solve everyday or specialized problems such as the G-forces of a roller coaster or the special effects of a themed attraction in a practical way. By picking up and reading this book, you are already on the road to the world of e-factor engineering.

Engineering entertainment is exciting and challenging work. You can let go of your imagination; catch that shooting star and freely dream of the impossible. Impossible today does not necessarily mean impossible tomorrow. You can concoct the strange, silly, serious, or daring and be considered an innovative leader, a model for other entertainment engineers to emulate.

> Consultancy on control system design for hotels, visitor centers, museums, and theme parks. Includes lighting, audio control systems, and complex interactive control. Systems integration, complete turnkey systems, assistance from specification to installation, commissioning and programming. U.S. based product sales and support for Maris Ltd.
>
> -Mad Systems

For more information on engineering careers, the differences between the branches of engineering, and how to select the right type of engineering for you, pick up a copy of *Is There an Engineer Inside You?* (Professional Publications, Inc. at www.ppi2pass.com)

Edwards Technologies, Inc. specializes in the design, engineering, fabrication and installation of audio, video, show control, interactives and software systems for theme parks, worlds fairs, museums, retail, restaurants and entertainment venues around the globe. Clients include: Universal, Warner Bros., Viacom, MGM, Disney, Fox, Ogden, LEGO, Coca-Cola, and Paramount Parks.

-Edwards Technologies, Inc.

Chapter Two

Merging Art and Science

Theme parks attempt to merge science and art to create illusion that is so close to reality that your mind and emotions cannot distinguish the reality from the magical. The idea with a theme park was to envelop the visitor in a seemingly different time and place based on stories.

Walt Disney opened Disneyland, the first themed park, on July 17th, 1955. Disneyland, being a themed park, was different from amusement parks because the entertainment in the attractions or rides was storytelling. A story told in a theme park strives to engage all five senses. A good story weaves a complex web completely immersing the viewer through sight, hearing, smelling, tasting, and feeling. A wonderful attraction can make us laugh and cry as we stand up to applaud an illusion that feels like reality.

Imagineering, a term coined by Walt Disney, refers to the work of a team of people who are responsible for the creation and development of all elements of a theme park. This unique team includes illustrators, architects, interior designers, landscape designers, machinists, writers, artists, researchers, schedulers, sound technicians, model-makers, film-makers, carpenters, estimators, accountants, industrial designers, graphic designers, and, of course, engineers. According to Nathan Naversen at ITEC Entertainment, "Engineers figure out a way to make it work. Whether it be sizing the structural columns and measuring shear forces on a roller coaster, or developing new electronics to make an animatronic character function. Engineers do the math to make everything 'stand up.' Structural

---

We design and manufacture animatronics, special effects, ride and show elements, show controls, robots, digital audio systems, animated figures for gaming casinos, theme parks, museums, restaurants and retail. We provide design, engineering and production services for lighting, scenery, audio, show design and concept development. Clients include Disney, NASA, FAO Schwarz, MGM, and Chuck E. Cheese.

-Garner Holt Productions, Inc.

and mechanical engineering are the most common majors."

How do they do it? Imagineers attempt to stimulate all five senses to transport the guest to the magical story-world they have created. The lines between illusion and reality overlap. The more senses that are enveloped simultaneously, the more real the created environment appears to be. To have a make-believe environment seem totally real, the technology behind it must be invisible. Art and science must blend into illusion. The imagineers know they have done their job well when their guests return again and again to see the magic they have created.

Appealing to the five senses is no easy task. A whole team of people may work together to appeal to only one aspect of one sense.

Feature Article – The Art of Accommodating All Five Senses

by Nathan Naversen

Like storytelling, illustration, or musical composition, the design of themed attractions is very much an art form. But it is much more complex because of the need to accommodate all five senses.

The medium of themed attraction entertainment is story telling, but the theme park attraction is different from any other medium of story telling known to the world. An artist's canvas may tell a story, yet it is limited in that it can only be seen. A story told in a motion picture or at a play is limited to sight and sound, but stories told at theme parks utilize all five senses to tell a convincing story. A good story has the ability to seemingly take a person on a journey to the ends of the earth, or beyond - and every possible technique should be used to accomplish this goal. In the following paragraphs, I will explain different methods of enhancing a themed environment in order to make a story seem more real.

Seeing is believing . . .

Visual imagery is the most obvious and most necessary tool for creating the themed environment. Each visitor will enter a themed attraction and then judge whether or not he believes what he sees. It is this critical judgment that the designer must try to positively influence. In doing so, it is imperative that every detail be thought out so that the created environment is perceived as real.

Here are several aspects that one needs to consider when creating the visual aspects of the themed attraction:

1. Architecture: The viewer should be completely engulfed in a new world, and the architecture should be designed to accomplish this task. In an ideal world, no expense should be spared to painstakingly recreate exquisite environments. Elements should be placed in the environment that reinforce the fact that this is indeed a special world, in contrast to what people are used to seeing in an ordinary world. For example, if we were designing a themed environment based on a medieval theme, the lighting might be provided by large flame torches or candelabras, the doors might be oversized, and the walls might be adorned with large tapestries. All of these props are elements that reinforce the idea that this is Camelot, not Medford, Oregon. Imagine straining to pull open a heavy timbered reinforced castle-keep door. What would such an experience immediately tell you about the environment you are in? In pulling on a door that is very different from the 3'x7' hollow core doors you are used to, the evidence of your location in a fantasy world should be immediately clear.

In the real world though, budgets have limits, so one cannot always recreate every detail down to the doorknob. But at the very least, one must always strive to avoid many common design pitfalls where some of the outside world "leaks" inside and diminishes the realism of the special world. A few examples of this include: exposed exit doors, places where a viewer can see behind a set, and allowing damage to the architecture to go unchecked.

A well-intentioned, but badly themed attraction can backfire. If shoddy architecture and special effects are designed the visitor may actually experience an attraction, thinking: "I'm sitting in a little battery powered buggy looking at plywood cutouts", instead of the true goal of the ride - to entertain and inspire with a wonderful or fantastic tale. A poorly themed attraction usually stimulates only one or two of the five senses, and very often it stimulates those senses either very poorly or in a detrimental fashion.

2. Landscape: All too often in today's theme parks, millions of dollars are spent on new attractions, and then the "icing on the cake" is left off. Landscape is to architecture what makeup is to a

model. Good landscape design adds an aesthetic to architecture that is necessary for completing an environment.

3. Lighting: The funny thing about lighting is that when it is done well, people generally comment on how good the architecture looks. However, when the lighting is done poorly, people are usually very quick to criticize the lighting design.

Lighting is very important to the success of a themed attraction. There are four primary types of lighting in themed entertainment design: architectural lighting, theatrical lighting, black lighting, and fiber optic lighting. Each has different functions, but very often two or more of these types of lighting are combined in a finished themed attraction.

Architectural lighting is the lighting that reveals common architectural interiors and exteriors, including the landscaping. Care should be taken to reveal the most important objects (called "tasks") in the area. This lighting consists of ordinary light fixtures and is used to guide the guests and make normal environments seem more pleasant or work easier.

Like dramatic productions, many themed attractions use theatrical sets to help tell a story. And when those sets are used, a special type of lighting is also commonly necessary. Theatrical lighting is used to create moods through the use of color and the careful highlighting of important elements on the set. Theatrical lights are extremely powerful units, often exceeding 1000 watts per fixture. They are an invaluable resource with almost limitless capabilities. Very often Gobo (short for go-between) patterns are used to project intricate patterns of light onto the walls, which is just one of the many special effects available with theatrical lighting.

Black lighting is used in various situations in themed environments to create striking visual effects. Black lights are special light bulbs that emit only Ultraviolet light radiation that is invisible to the human eye. Special fluorescent paints glow when bombarded with this ultraviolet light, which is how the effect is created. For example, black light could be used to create the illusion of a far off city at night. In this example, the distant windows and streetlights are painted on a scenic backdrop with fluorescent paints and the black light would create a glowing effect. Black lighting is also useful when lighting three-dimensional animated characters, as they appear life like and cartoon-ish. As well, a room becomes extremely striking in appearance when lit only with black light, as people are not used to seeing fluorescence. Indeed, black lighting is a valuable tool in certain situations.

Fiber optic lighting has gone from a little used resource a few years ago to a widespread lighting technique with a tremendous number of applications today. A fiber optic light is composed of an illuminator, which produces light to be directed into the fibers, and bundles of plastic tubes (the fibers themselves in various lengths and sizes). Fiber optic lighting looks exactly like neon lighting with two distinct advantages: first, it is flexible tubing so it can be moved while it is illuminated; and second, its color can be changed (sometimes every few seconds) through the use of a color wheel that is attached to the illuminator. A further advantage is that the end points of the fibers make realistic looking stars for settings where a nighttime sky is needed, or it can be used to make ordinary signage sparkle. Fiber optics can be used for lighting while simultaneously shooting security camera footage as light travels both directions through the fibers. The only drawbacks to fiber optics are that the bundles of fibers tend to cost about 20 dollars per linear foot (imagine covering an entire ceiling with "stars" at that cost), and that they generate a tremendous amount of heat.

Sound: The mood setter

There is no more effective tool for shaping the mood in a space than sound. Consider the feelings you experienced when you last heard the following movie theme songs: Raiders of the Lost Ark; title song for Star Wars "Imperial Death March"; The Twilight Zone; The theme song for Psycho; The Theme Song for Disney's Pinocchio, "When You Wish Upon a Star"; and Rocky, "Eye of the Tiger."

In many respects, these popular movie theme songs are just as recognizable as the movies themselves, if not more so. Just as no television show or movie would go without background music, the power of sound should never be neglected as a mood-enhancing tool for themed attractions either. Sound is all-important, whether it is musical theme songs, special effects or story enhancing dialogue. Too, sound should always be over-utilized rather than under-utilized. Sometimes, silence is desired, and in such cases it should be used to punctuate the drama of a situation, but never because "we just couldn't think of something to do there." Just as television and movies continuously use background sounds to add mood and interest, so should it be with themed attractions and architectural showplaces.

The next time you visit Disney's Animal Kingdom, be sure to pay attention to the relaxing mood music continuously played in several key areas of the park, especially near the front ticket gate. In my opinion, the music helped contribute to a relaxing themed experience even on the most crowded days. Indeed, I visited Animal Kingdom on a day when they set an attendance record, yet I noticed that I did not feel stressed out like I would normally under those circumstances. I attributed my relaxed mood that day in part to the presence of the background music.

Tactile Tactics...

Tactile stimulation is important in theme rides as well. It is less important than sound effects in terms of overall impact to the guest, but it still can be a very important tool in enhancing the "realness" of an environment. Consider the effect a spray of mist on the face would have on a guest in a tropical themed adventure ride, or how the cold iron bars in a dungeon might feel to a visitor of that attraction. The applications for texture planning are endless, and clearly contribute to an effective environmental design.

Interestingly enough, the most effective torture method known to the world today is a technique called sensory depravation. When used, the victim is placed inside a seamless silicon full body suit, where he can feel or touch absolutely nothing. He is suspended in a weightless water environment with earplugs, an eye visor and a muzzle. After several hours without any sensory input whatsoever, the victim becomes hypersuggestable to any sensory input, (namely, the interrogator's suggestion that the victim answer his questions). But just as the power of touch is used to torture spies, experts agree that a mother's loving touch is just as important to the positive development of a healthy baby. Clearly, though overlooked, meaningful tactile input is a very necessary factor in our lives, and it should be considered in theme attraction design as well.

A Taste Sensation. . .

Although smell and taste are usually thought of as two different senses, they are so closely linked that for our purposes they can be considered the same. Humans use these senses very little in comparison to those senses previously mentioned, but they should never be overlooked when planning an attraction. Indeed, a well-placed scent can provide that final touch of realism that will make the experience a memorable one. Consider how the smell of smoke could enhance a burning building set, or how that distinctive sea aroma would contribute to an ocean themed attraction. Imagine how the wafting smell of rain (accomplished by adding nitrogen content to the air) would make a visitor feel before entering a ride featuring a tornado or thunderstorm? There are many more uses of smell than are immediately obvious to most, but good designers get paid to focus on details like these.

One final note about smell and taste. A few years ago I was touring a Disney theme park when I noticed a popcorn cart and an attendant. I approached him and asked him what affect the "popcorn smell" had on his sales. His reply was enlightening. He said, "Every time I turn on my artificial popcorn smell, I can have a line of up to ten people within five minutes." At the time, he and I were the only ones there, and not surprisingly, he had his "smell button" turned off.

The best themed attractions can be said to be perfect mimics of the environment it attempts to recreate. When done well, the lines between fantasy and reality are blurred, and a truly memorable guest experience is created. But to be effective, these attractions must effectively stimulate all five senses. *Nathan Naversen is a themed attraction designer currently residing in Orlando, Florida.*

Now that we know how to stimulate all five senses, let's focus our attention back to other aspects of entertainment engineering. E-factor engineering can

Parsons is a full service A-E/CM firm with offices worldwide. The Entertainment Group is located in Pasadena, CA. With key partners, Parsons provides single point responsibility for themed entertainment project development from concept through design construction and turn over of operations. Experience base includes theme parks, resorts, hotels, retail and dining.
                    -Parsons Infrastructure and Technology

include but is not limited to designing, building, conceiving, producing or orchestrating environments such as theme parks, themed retail stores, themed restaurants, sports facilities, museums, aquariums, zoos, casinos, cinemas, expos, recreational facilities, coliseums, and planetariums.

To become successful at designing entertainment we must begin by knowing and understanding the audience. We must know what turns them on, we must appreciate their mental state, and we must deliver quality content. Today, people have many avenues available to them for their entertainment. Individuals want and have access to more than ever before. The Internet has opened the world to the average consumer and entertainment can be only a few mouse clicks away.

As a designer, you not only have to get them out of the house and away from their home entertainment, you must get them to spend their entertainment dollars on your event.

Holmes & Narver is a full service architectural and engineering firm experienced in the renovation, retheming and development of new attractions at major theme parks. We work as an extension of the client's design team or with other concept and show designers and specialize in turning their concepts into details…to help them put on the show!

-Holmes & Narver

THEME PARK DESIGN SOFTWARE

To get in entertainment design mode and also get some practice and simulated experience thinking about what goes into designing a theme park, pick up a copy of Sim Theme Park. Sim Theme Park is a theme park simulation software that lets you design, build, and manage your own theme park. You are in charge of every decision, from the design of the roller coaster to the price of hamburgers.

Playing Sim Theme Park, you will find that designing great rides is not enough. You must always be researching better rides, adding to the theme of the park, hiring and firing the staff, setting the admission prices, and even adjusting the merchandise and concessions. To supplement park income, players can build shops and setup side-shows. Every aspect of running the park is at your fingertips.

Designing theme parks is no easy task. In the article, *Theme Parks by Generation X,* Bob Rogers says, "Once you have the crowd gathered, it's back to the same

Production Arts is a full-service lighting rental, sales and service organization. They are dealers for all major theatrical lighting manufacturers, plus sales and large turnkey installations. Exclusive distributors for Robert Juliat fixtures, E/T/C Audiovisual projection, Avenger show control systems and Ludwig Pani distributor and service center. A Production Resource Group Company.
                                    -Production Arts Lighting

fundamentals that have been apart of every successful entertainment: You still need to make them laugh, charm them, dazzle them, take them somewhere new and different, give them a chance to be a part of the crowd, to see and be seen, feed them well, take great care of them, and make them feel better about themselves and the world."

One of the major benefits of using this software as an introduction to the mind set of designing theme parks is that when you complete your park, you can publish it on the Internet and compare it to other players parks. You can even chat with the creators of the other published parks and maybe learn a few tricks and secrets.

Chatting with other players is a great opportunity to network with other aspiring theme park designers. Find out what people all over the world are doing to prepare for this career. You can exchange contacts, employment resources, and inside information. Use the tips, tricks, resources and contacts to make yourself competitive in the marketplace. The more information

Setpoint's business is in providing high quality engineered systems, designs and solutions to select amusement and automation customers. We provide innovative multi-discipline engineering expertise in ride system design, analysis, and fabrication. Our core expertise is in quick execution of tough electro-mechanical projects and the ability to manage, track and report projects in a highly effective manner.
                              -Setpoint Engineered Systems, Inc.

you obtain and the more visible you become, the more employable you will be. Visit their website at http://www.simthemepark.com and see for yourself.

CREATE A MODEL

Another great step, something you should do immediately, is to take the story you wrote out on a napkin, wallpaper, or put on your computer and make it into a physical entity by creating a model. If you have foam, clay, or wood, you can make a 3-D model of your idea. The model can help your idea take shape, and it

A more recent model created by CMG Models for the
IAAPA Tradeshow.

will show you what you have not thought of yet. Model-making is one of the most important steps in the attraction evolution of themed entertainment. Sometimes, by creating the model, your project may end up as something completely different than what you first imagined. The ability to view the project from all sides and observe the way the pieces fit together is the only way to get the whole story. The Imagineers at Disney are said to have several model shops encompassing 80,000 square feet of space!

CMG Models, a roller coaster model shop, creates wooden models of roller coasters before parks such as Busch Gardens or Magic Mountain commit to spending millions of dollars on the fabrication of a coaster. "I got started making models when I was in high school; I would debut roller coaster models at the art shows at school every year. It was a lot of fun debuting a new coaster every year, and soon it became expected by fellow students and teachers. Over the years my modeling skills have improved with experience

Scenery West offers complete design, fabrication, installation and themed construction services for museums, parks, attractions, hotels, casinos and retail stores worldwide. Our in-house design and production expertise is drawn from 25 years of service to the film, television and themed entertainment industries. SW also offers a variety of materials through its product catalog.

-Scenery West

and a growing knowledge of roller coasters. I can account for some of my successes by just being in the right place at the right time," said Chris Gray, founder of CMG Models. See the article by Chris Gray on how to make a roller coaster model in chapter five.

Merging art and science to create amazing theme parks is different than engineering in any other medium. The end result of your attractions are people oriented rather than technology oriented. Engineers love to fully harness the capabilities of technology, but in this industry, along with the perfectly executed animatronic characters and innovative technology, the guest experience must always come first.

Design and fabrication of exhibits, displays, themed restaurants and museums.
                                                -1220 Exhibits

Chapter Three

Create A Compelling Story

According Bob Rogers of BRC Imagination Arts, The Lion King "was the number one, single most valuable and profitable entertainment project, of any kind, created last year" (June 13, 1995, TiLE Conference). However, people did not come to see the abundant special effects or how the imagineers created the film, "they came to see a great story, beautifully told, with lovable, interesting, and engaging characters," said Rogers.

The Lion King took in over $742 million in its first nine months from movie theaters, over 30 million videos have been sold, and there are numerous character licenses, TV versions, park attractions, Broadway Shows, and Ice Shows. When all the figures are tallied, "The Lion King will undoubtedly become the most profitable film ever made," said Rogers.

To create a lasting impression as your story unfolds, events must be magical. According to Jack Rouse, CEO of Jack Rouse Associates, "Events engage people at a point which transcends the essence of the product or corporation that is

sponsoring or creating the event." Rouse went on to say to a different group, "It comes down to research. It comes down to knowing them, not as customers – certainly not if you're talking in any way about entertainment. But rather seeing the users of our developments as audiences whose attention we must engage and whose mindset we must earn, rather than as customers to whom we are selling products."

Engineering Consultant specializing in Themed Entertainment Video Imaging, Audio & Control Systems, Video Post Production Systems, Film/Video Interface Techniques, Video Disk Technology, High Quality Imaging Systems, Specialized Transmission Systems, & Product Design & Manufacturing Procedures.
   -Gary E. Thompson, Television Engineering Services

Imagine going to a theme park and riding a <u>Lion King</u> attraction. The attraction may go through a beautiful jungle. You may see other lions, elephants, zebras, and a host of other animals from the movie. It may recreate scenes from the footage to make you relive moments in Simba's life. You may watch him wrestle with Nala as a cub, and you may watch him become king again. Because the film tells such a great story, the attraction is accordingly compelling.

Now imagine that you did not know the <u>Lion King</u> story and had never heard of the movie. What would that do to your experience of the attraction? You may ride through the attraction and see some animals in a beautiful jungle, but with no story behind it, your experience will not memorable.

Feature Article - Guest Experience Rules!

by Peter iNova

Rule #1 - It's the Guest, the Whole Guest, and Nothing But the Guest

The nature of an attraction can be nearly anything. It can be as small as a shop or as large as a theme park. It can sell you, feed you, please you, thrill you or give you a chance to win. No matter what it does, your guest is the customer that gives it a reason to exist in the first place.

That individual will arrive at your entrance bringing a lifetime of experiences, knowledge, information, cultural myths and beliefs along with them. Recognizing this, Guest Experience designers can predict certain things about the guest and start channeling the experience towards a positive goal.

Rule #2 - Precondition me.

Guests arrive with so much in the way of extraneous mental baggage, not to mention camcorders, kids and a stroller, that no individual state of mind shows up perfectly prepared for your attraction the way you might wish.

An arsenal of tools and techniques exists to change all this. Architecture, service, involvement, distraction, interaction, attention to detail and solutions to predictable problems all can conspire to put guests in a particularly good mood. Accommodating wheel chairs is now appropriately mandatory, accommodating valuables, kids and strollers can be a good thing, too.

Whether the decor is authentic, impressionistic or in between, a certain portion of the audience may take delight in showing their friends how fake it is.

Rule #3 - Thou Shalt Not Bewilder.

Never allow the guest to become needlessly confused. You may, for dramatic purposes misdirect, build anticipation, keep them guessing, startle them or make it impossible for people to predict what's coming next, but if you do something that leaves them lost and drifting, you will be losing comfort points in the Guest Experience.

Rule #4 - Model. Model. Model.

Today it is common to make physical models of architectural elements but new technologies make it possible to actually walk through a proposed design before the plans are anywhere near final and before a physical model is ever made. This is the new capability of Venue Simulation and it is such a useful tool that it changes the very way complex ideas are planned and refined.

If this article has a basic useful new idea that you have not heard elsewhere, this is it: Venue Simulation solves problems, saves money, demonstrates ideas and makes better thought out attractions possible.

The Immersive Media Center is an example of how Guest Experience goes beyond the final ticket paying customer. To us, the developer of an attraction is the guest and the experience that individual or group encounters is its own form of Guest Experience.

Rule #5 - Magic Happens. Make it so.

Guests arrive willing to suspend their disbelief. To a point. They will, under certain circumstances, allow violations of reality:

- A projection in place of a live situation.

- A well presented theatrical effect in place of a dangerous reality.

- An environment that is out of scale.

- A physical phenomenon that is ordinarily impossible.

- A ghost that is convincingly real.

- Magic.

- Spectacle.

Everyone knows magic can happen under controlled circumstances. Since all attractions are controlled circumstances, it follows that anything that distracts from the magic is a bad thing. The magic is the sum total of the special quality that makes your attraction a "Must See" or "WOW" experience. Bonus points are given by guests according to a set chart of responses:

utterance		points	implication
Gee	=	1	None. No impact. Anything can get a "Gee".
Gosh	=	2	A few extra customers show up Saturday.
Hey!	=	3	Several extra customers heard about it, trickled in.
Omigosh!	=	5	Customers tell their friends. Who tell theirs.
Wow!	=	8	Customers tell everybody they meet. Loudly.
Holy Cow!!	=	10	Stockholders covered. Career covered. Yess!

Your results may vary. Local slang can modify the response names. There is a negative scale, but we don't even want to go there.

The magic that happens in your attraction will be as carefully placed there by good design, original concept and vision as it is by technical integrity, high quality media and superior physical execution.

I feel that these two phases, dreaming up the magic and actually taking the responsibility to build it, are not things that can be given to two separate groups. The latter won't have the vision so they will make compromises without a deep understanding of the mission, the first won't need to take responsibility for making the vision practical so they will sell you anything that pleases you. I've seen it happen all over the world.

What you really want is a team of people that include the vision, technology, craftsmanship and responsibility to make it happen. The rule might be better phrased as "magic happens through teamwork."

Rule #6 - Hide Something.

Surprise, novelty, originality and comedy are carefully channeled elements in superior Guest Experiences. Preconditioning can set up one expectation that is transcended by the unexpected. Smiles and laughter are money in the bank. The worse thing that can be done is to tell guests exactly what is going to happen and then have that come true exactly on schedule.

In the best crafted attractions the surprises are so thick and plentiful that people leave with the feeling that they couldn't have seen it all in a single visit.

When the surprises are inelegantly orchestrated, rule #3 takes over.

The opposite of hiding is revealing. Rule #6B is "Reveal something."

Rule #7 - Show me the money.

The guest is thinking:

- Immerse me in something I couldn't have dreamed up on my own.

- Make me believe I've gone somewhere and some *when*...

- Show me the money.

- Make me feel like you spared no expense to delight me.

- Don't EVER let me see you cutting items out of the budget, for I am the Guest and I am strictly not interested in seeing how on my behalf.

Remember that as soon as attraction designers say "All we have to do is..." all the Guest has to do is tell their friends "You didn't miss anything."

Rule #8 - It only exists if it works.

If it's supposed to work, make sure it is working RIGHT NOW! The guest sees every non-functioning element through a filter that is constantly whispering, "I don't have all day and I may never pass this way again."

That little sign you post outside your attraction that tells folks which ride or show isn't operating today - for whatever reason - is what your first grade teacher told you never to give her, an excuse.

Rule #9 - Let me take it with me.

Of course, nearly every attraction has its version of a souvenir shop and retail opportunities, but today the world of guests carries camcorders as standard equipment. (Note to retail outlet and gift shop buyers: Stock every conceivable format of film and video tape, even a few of those cassettes the pros use, they run out, too.)

No image carried home on a video camcorder will have anywhere near the impact as being there, which is exactly what the guest will say over and over to his friends as he narrates the video of his visit to your attraction.

This is good for you. Guests with video camera are not ripping you off, stealing your attraction's thunder and taking it back home to show their friends how bad it was. In fact, if the attraction isn't thunderful, they won't even bother to show the tape at all. Allowing people to video tape inside your attraction is good word-of-mouth advertising. It's just a mouth with a lens in it.

Rule #10 - Say Thank You. And mean it.

What kind of thank you? A clever sign, a mailed special offer, a coupon, a refreshing vista, a little joke, one more clever display... any of these may do the job. Dumping the guest into the cheapest looking exit probably won't.

You may be thankful the guest spent time and money with you, but the key here is that the Guest must

ITEC is a full service entertainment design company developing shows, attractions, entertainment complexes, resorts, miniature golf, graphics & signage, special effects, and technical show control systems.
                                        -ITEC Entertainment Corp., Inc.

understand that you meant it. Now that would be a good experience. *Reprinted courtesy of Peter iNova, Creative Director of Metavision.*

Engineers who work in the entertainment field are some of the most creative people in the world. Constantly attempting to create the impossible, this line of work is thrilling and certainly not in keeping with the ancient pocket-protector, anti-social nerd stereotype of engineers. These engineers frequently apply modified design principles to accomplish an effect that was conjured by the creative team. They are the bottom-line, the ones who have to figure out how to transcend reality.

Transcending reality is dependent on technology but technology is not the only tool you must have in your box. Bob Rogers of BRC Imagination Arts said, "Technology does, however, have one very important role to play. And that's to help you gather a crowd.

Full service lighting design provided through all phases of project design and development in support of architectural, show and theatrical lighting design needs. Concept development, design documents, construction coordination, programming and maintenance documentation are services provided to conceive, develop, construct and maintain an exciting lighting environment.

-Gallegos Lighting Design

Technology very frequently gives you that nice one liner, 'on a screen five stories tall' or 'filmed and projected at 60 frames per second' or what have you. Phrases like these allow you to intrigue and attract an audience so that you gather a whole bunch of eager faces there waiting to see your show. Indeed, that audience may be totally charmed and dazzled by that technology all by itself – for about two minutes. But then you must transcend the limits of that technology and put on a presentation they'll remember."

In addition to creating the memorable, the attractions designed by the engineer must be able to stand-up to considerable wear and tear. The ride or attraction will be restarted every few minutes everyday for possibly many years to come. In addition, the attraction must surpass the rigorous safety standards of the industry. According to Bruce Johnson, a Disney Imagineer, "The statistics are against us. Think about it. If there is a one in a million chance something will go wrong, and ten million guests ride our ride, then something will happen ten times. We can't design to

Lucci & Associates provides electrical engineering for theme parks and attractions. We provide interface drawings for show control, audio, pyro, video, lighting and similar systems. We also provide facility and show electrical plans for any venue in the enterainment industry.

-Lucci & Associates

that one in a million. We have to design to one in hundreds of millions."

Once you create a compelling story, focus on the guest experience and adhere to the required safety standards, you are well on your way to creating fabulous entertainment. Communicate your ideas regularly and don't be afraid to use new technology, try different approaches or apply suggestions for improvements.

> We provide simple, cost effective solutions to the multitude of technical and business problems associated wth producing a themed attraction.
> -Solutions for Engineering & Business

Chapter Four

Preparing For Your Career

Now that you are convinced you want to design themed entertainment, how do you prepare for this career? What will you do on a daily basis? You think you would love to work at Disney, but is that your only option?

Choosing a Company

Disney is the biggest employer of themed designers and certainly a great company to work for.

However, there are loads of other theme parks, entertainment design companies, and leisure time facilities such as Universal Studios, Busch Gardens, Paramount Parks, and Premiere Parks. The appendix of this book is full of the names and employment contacts of companies that design themed entertainment including but not limited to theme parks, aquariums, zoos, cinemas, restaurants, and sporting events. Before choosing, think about who you are, what conditions you may prefer to work under, and your strengths and weaknesses.

If you want to work at a company that employs thousands of people, such as Disney, you need to become an expert at just one thing. Alternatively, if you want to work at a company that only employs 25 to 30 people, you might want to become a generalist and learn to do several things very well. Either way, you will be working in teams and need to be able to communicate very effectively. According to Will Pedersen, the director of engineering for Rando Productions, "The most

---

Established in 1978, AVG, Inc. designs, develops, manufactures and installs high tech, computer controlled audio/animatronic figures and show presentations, interactive product displays, dark rides and special effects for the theme park, themed entertainment, leisure, retail, special events, motion picture and television industries.

-AVG, Inc.

creative and best ideas are a result of teamwork, not one man shows." This is no place for prima donnas!

Communication and patience are valuable assets when mixing teams of people to develop themed entertainment. Engineers must be able to communicate with everyone from the landscaper to the artist to the architect to the stage hand. "You need to have patience with creative artistic people. Engineers want to solve the problem now!" said Pedersen.

One of the largest independent designers and producers of themed attractions in the world is ITEC Entertainment. The company was started 13 years ago by former Walt Disney imagineering cast members who came to realize that no one was creating highly themed, highly entertaining attractions for the "rest of the world."

Feature Article - A Day in the Life of an Imagineer

by Nathan Naversen

Brainstorming: Quite possibly the most fun part of the job. Brainstorming sessions are also called *blue sky* exercises because the sky is the limit is what can be suggested at these meetings. In a brainstorming session, we come up with a creative solution for a design problem. As Walt Disney once said, *"If you focus on the long shot, it makes the close-ups easier."* Once we have a good concept complete, we can then move to creating the fun little details that make each attraction so wonderful to enjoy.

Illustration: It is important to be able to express one's ideas on paper because very often the only way of explaining an idea is to illustrate it. At ITEC, a high emphasis is placed on being able to "talk with a pencil". Generally, most of the concept illustration occurs after the brainstorming ends and before the architectural design work begins.

Design and Layout: Themed process begins. Detailing is a long process, yet extremely important. Detailing is how you explain exactly how a particular space or item is to look and feel. The true key to theming is good detail work, or to quote the old cliché, *The devil is in the details!* At ITEC, we will often detail every wall, nook, cranny, prop, awning, and ceiling grate to create the look we are after. Each detail is drawn to scale with measurements and specifications so that it may be fabricated.

Drafting: Drafting is where much of the design time is spent. The process often requires hours of time in front of a computer and on the drawing board, drafting and re-drafting plans for our designs.   It is this long refinement process that turns a pretty picture into something that can be built and experienced.   The end result: 500 pounds of blueprints and lots of happy, smiling families.

These are just a few of the big tasks I do each week, although hours of research, meetings, and site visits are also often a very big part of my job in the creative group as well. Attraction design requires many other specialties that I have not mentioned, but I hope this gives you a good idea about what I do at work each day. *Nathan Naversen is a themed attraction designer currently residing in Orlando, Florida.*

When considering developing skills to become a theme park or entertainment engineer, consult the want ads to see what type of jobs are being offered, and focus your development efforts on the skills needed by employers in the themed entertainment industry. The following are two job postings that were available when this book was being written. They are good examples of the required skills and needs of theme park employers.

"Use your Engineering Degree to Entertain Millions."

Universal Studios is bringing our wildly popular, movie-based theme parks to Japan. Our newest park, situated on 144 acres of Osaka's waterfront, features 18 exciting attractions patterned after those in our US parks, including rides, live shows and a behind-the-scenes look at the magic of movie making. There are also three brand new attractions designed to thrill and entertain Japanese audiences. As we continue our expansion, we have the following opportunity:

October 29, 1999
AUDIO VISUAL ENGINEER

Get out of your world and into a whole new universe of entertainment at Universal Studios Theme Park in Osaka. You'll be a part of the Parkwide Ride and Show System, bringing sights and sounds to a large multi-faceted theme park opening in 2001. You'll manage the development and organization of the audio, video and projection systems for each show, as well as develop and oversee project schedules and budgetary requirements.

To do this, you'll need 5-7 years of combined audio-video design and development experience, along with 2-3 years of project management in an entertainment-related environment. Knowledge of the latest audio, video, and film projection technologies, software and control systems, and AutoCAD systems is also required, along with excellent organizational, analytical, and communication skills. Master's or the equivalent experience in Engineering or related field is mandatory, as is proficiency in Microsoft Office applications.

August 5, 1999
RIDE ENGINEER

This position is at Universal Studios Japan, and is responsible for managing the design and development of ride systems and their ancillary equipment from inception through opening day. This engineer must be an active participant in the design, production, and installation of the ride system, and will be responsible for all vendor and contractor issues, budgets, schedules and team coordination.

We are looking for a person with a Bachelors Degree in Engineering (preferably Mechanical) or 4 yrs equivalent, a minimum 3+ yrs of engineering and project management experience, and experience with turnkey projects in the entertainment/theme park field. We prefer an engineer with supervisory and contractor/vendor management experience, as well as experience in component selection and detailed machine design. This position requires excellent written and verbal skills, knowledge of AutoCAD, computer modeling, Microsoft Access and all programs in Microsoft Office. Familiarity with international business is highly advantageous."

-Job descriptions listed at TAC Entertainment Staffing

Projex International is a specialty contractor with emphasis in themed environments for amusement parks, casinos, hotels, nightclubs, restaurants, and retail stores worldwide. Services include: design research, engineering, metal and mechanical fabrication, sculpting, moldmaking, scenic elements in wood, fiberglass, and plastic, painting, transportation, and installation.

-Projex International

Dave Graul of Attraction Services says the most important skills an engineering student can acquire before canvassing the industry with resumes is CAD skills, PLC programming, and people skills. He further suggests, "Get experience working on projects and hardware at school or home. Build a network of contacts and be persistent. Show employers that you have a genuine interest in the industry."

CO-OPS AND INTERNSHIPS

Cooperative education or a co-op experience is one where an engineering student alternates work experience in government, industry or business with academics. For example, a student may do a parallel co-op where they work part-time and go to school part-time or complete a traditional co-op where they work for six months and go to school for six months. Robert McDonnell of Tilden Lobnitz and Cooper said he participated in a co-op program at Rochester Institute of Technology. He was fortunate to work on a variety of

> Scharff Weisberg, Inc. provides design & engineering services for audio/video installations with a specialty in large screen display and show control applications. Services include conceptual design, integration, documentation, installation, testing, programming, and maintaince.
> -Scharff Weisberg, Inc.

projects, and his success has continued on for over sixteen years.

Because a co-op program is longer, the experience you obtain can be more meaningful. Additionally, a co-op experience can show employers you have experience and a solid desire to work in the entertainment field. In today's competitive market, you need to do everything possible to make sure you are the shining star.

Engineering internships are another way to get your foot in the door. They generally consist of a summer job related to your major at an engineering company. David Tanaka of Industrial Light and Magic began his successful career by interning every summer. By the time he graduated, he was the first choice when a position became available.

As technology increases, engineers need to become more versatile, adaptable and social. Luckily, schools everywhere are changing their curriculums to include more teamwork and public speaking. Both the

A full service turnkey custom theming group specializing in creating elements/environments with impact. Services include: design, development, engineering, fabrication, project management, construction and installation. We specialize in the fabriction of models, sets, props, prototypes, replicas, sculpting and mold making. Industry experience includes retail, exhibit, aerospace, museum, theater, airport and hotel.

-Penwal Industries, Inc.

previous want ads called for excellent written and verbal communication skills, and that is the best first step you can take toward developing the necessary skills to land a job as a themed attraction engineer. Read through several other job postings and begin to learn the most commonly sought after software packages such as Microsoft Office, Microsoft Project, and AutoCAD. With perseverance, talent, enthusiasm, a winning attitude, excellent interpersonal skills, and a growing knowledge about the theme park industry, you will eventually get your dream job. According to Don Hilsen, an Imagineer at Disney, "Any ride engineer can design parts. But it is a unique kind of engineer who can blend a creative story and theme with practical technology. To continue to rise to the standard setting challenge as a ride engineer here, you have to be more than a nuts and bolts type of person. You have to be a big thinker, a 'blank sheet of paper' person."

As newer technology becomes more sophisti-cated, the demand for creative engineers will only in-

---

Special effects company specializing in high-tech mechanical effects, flame effects, atmospheric effects, animatronics and custom props. We also provide entertainment engineering services as they relate to dynamic mechanical systems, electrical systems/ controls, specialty ride vehicles and structural systems. All fabrication is completed in our 50,000 square foot facility in Valencia.

-Attraction Services

crease. In November 1998, TAC Entertainment Staffing was launched to meet the growing demand for engineering and creative talent. TAC entertainment online is the biggest compilation of entertainment industry specific jobs, and you can even submit your resume.

Visit them at http://www.tacentertainment.com or http://www.ShowBizJobs.com in the technical hanger.

ESSENTIAL SKILLS

According to Richard Graham, president of Projex International, the most important skills an engineering student can acquire are, "a solid knowledge in the basics and how to apply standard formulas to the combination of unconventional materials and structures. Nothing is usually ever repeated in this business."

In a November/December 1997 interview in Graduating Engineer and Computer Careers magazine, Mike King, a software engineer for Walt Disney Feature Animation (WDFA) said that in 1995, after deciding he would never forgive himself for not trying to get a job in

Oceaneering's Entertainment Systems (OES) provides stand alone and turn-key services for the entertainment industry - concept development, engineering, production and installation. Field Services include system repair, maintenance, refurbishment, and diagnostics. OES specializes in underwater and land systems, medium/large dynamic mechanical systems, Show Action Equipment (SAE) and specialized ride systems.

-Oceaneering Entertainment Systems

computer graphics, he launched a job search spanning several months which included networking via email with those already in the industry, sending resumes, and reading up on the graphics industry. Following many rejections, mainly because he lacked experience, Disney called. That's when timing kicked in. "My timing was good because 1995 heralded the recent boom in the computer animation industry, so I managed to catch the beginning of the wave," says King.

Imagineers are not the only type of engineer that a theme park such as Disney, Busch Gardens, or Universal Studios requires. Themed parks also need industrial engineers, ride and show engineers, project engineers, architectural engineers, electrical engineers, computer engineers, mechanical engineers, structural engineers, and/or audio/video engineers. Imagineers may design the face of what the public sees, but other engineers are also needed to support the business of theme parks such as crowd control, research and development, training, and equipment maintenance.

Independent control systems engineer specializing in themed entertainment projects. Experienced in show control, motion base, motion control, and fire systems projects. Hardware design and fabrication, software programming, and system documentation services available. Consulting services also available in maintenance management and periodic inspection procedures.

-Canton Consulting Group

Chapter Five

According to a 1997 roller coaster census, there were 871 operating coasters worldwide.

Roller Coaster Design

No discussion on themed entertainment would be complete without at least a mention of roller coaster design. Roller coasters are in many theme parks and of primary concern to aspiring designers. When asked the question, "If you could design any ride in a theme park, what would it be?" Most of us thrillseekers inevitably choose the biggest, baddest and most exhilarating ride imaginable. We begin with roller coasters.

Click-clack up the hill it goes to drop into a death defying corkscrew roll. The machine has us out of our seat and screaming our confessions so that this thrill may not be taken away from us. The most famous coasters are referred to by terms like Scream Machine and given names such as Atom Smasher, Mind Bender, Cyclone, Beast, Steel Phantom, Thunderbolt, and Giant Dipper, and with good reason.

In the year 2000, coasters are being built bigger, faster and more intense than ever. Parks now have 30 different types of coasters to choose from and are adding them by the handful.

According to an April 2000 interview in Park World Magazine, "Advancements in technology are allowing manufacturers to build new and unique types of coasters which give theme parks unlimited choices when shopping for the next great marketable attraction," observes Jim Seay, president of Premier Rides. "Theme parks are buying coasters because it is smart business. It has been proven time and time again that new coasters quickly pay for themselves and bolster annual

Provides consultant services in theater design, projection engineering for film and video systems, and the design engineering of special projection screens.
-Sigma Design Group

attendance. The average attendance at parks that added Premier Rides coasters in 1999 was up 43 percent. That is a strong statement for the business side of introducing new roller coasters."

In 1998, 300 million people descended on amusement parks to experience thrills achievable in no other way. We want to be hurled around the track at incredible speeds; we want to be terrified and we want to have fun in complete safety. When the ride is over,

Montu - a steel-track inverted looping coaster at Busch Gardens in Tampa, Florida

we rush back into line to do it again. Enthusiasts are constantly in search of steeper hills, more G's, tighter rolls, and more airtime.

ROLLER COASTER HISTORY

Roller coasters have been around since the 1800s. The first roller coaster ride in the United States was a gravity-powered mine-train. The Mauch Chunk Railway in the mountains of Pennsylvania became a full-time attraction after the mine shut down. The crowds lined up, paid a nickel, and were sent down the tracks at a whooping six miles per hour. Mules then pulled the coaster back up the hill and shared the ride down with the thrillseekers.

The 1920s were the golden age of roller coasters. Improved safety and design techniques made for more exhilarating rides. The coasters could go faster, the hills were getting larger, and the curves were getting tighter. By 1929, there were 3000 operating roller coasters in the world.

During the Great Depression, amusement parks suffered along with all recreational activities, and because of low park attendance, most park owners could not afford to keep up the maintenance of the coasters, and most were torn down or abandoned. By 1960, there were fewer than 200 coasters remaining in the United States.

On July 17, 1955, Walt Disney revived amusement parks by opening Disneyland. In 1959, Disneyland had the first steel-tracked coaster, Matterhorn Bobsled Ride. Designers were elated with the strength of steel compared to wood. Twists, turns and other thrills not possible with wood coasters were to become the norm as crowds flocked to experience "the rush."

Today, roller coaster design is all about what the human body can withstand. The Steel Phantom and Fujiyama reach lightning speeds of 85 m.p.h., a new coaster, Millenium Force, released in May 2000, will reach 92 m.p.h., and Superman Kryton Coaster, the world's tallest and fastest floorless coaster, reaches 70m.p.h..

Roller coaster designs may take 2 or 3 years to complete and cost as much as $8 million. The design of coasters is now done on computer using CAD systems and the safety of riding has increased considerably. CAD systems can design the layout as well as the calculate the forces and stresses on riders and the ride itself.

Earlier we talked about the importance of making models to get the entire picture. Chris Gray founder of CMG Models, a roller coaster scale model company says, "one advantage of building models is that the client can see the ride or the structure before it's complete. This gives the marketing team something to go with, to build anticipation for the ride or building. To see the excitement in someone's eyes when they see what's coming is an awesome sight. Other advantages are putting the model into the site of the actual project using digital pictures of the models and of the site. This lets one see how it's going to look when it is complete in the park. Now days, people are asking for computer

> Using themed environments for corporate communications creating "Corporate Land" and "Brand Land." Design/concept development for world's fairs, visitor centers. Theming, storytelling for themed entertainment.
>
> -Arthesia

generated models so they can also take a ride on the coaster before it is complete."

Feature Article - Roller Coaster Model Design

by Chris Gray

I have been pursuing a career in the amusement industry since I was a child. It all started with riding old push lawn mowers over the hills in eastern Kentucky. I started building roller coaster models in high school and would debut them at the school's art show every year. Since then I have traveled all over the world with the U.S. Navy developing my construction skills as a welder. Two weeks after my discharge, I started on the Gwazi Model for Busch Gardens, Tampa Bay. I placed a bid for the project to Busch Gardens and backed it up with pictures of my older models. Two weeks later I was commissioned.

Theming Architects, General Contractors, Theming Fabricators. Our artists, craftsmen, design and project leaders provide fabrication, installation, general construction, and themed architecture for clients worldwide.

-Nassal Company, The

Gwazi was a very complex coaster. I had never seen anything like it before. During the construction I learned new skills such as how to bank a track and how to track curves on a wooden coaster model. Banking track is where the track is tilted laterally. This allows the train to turn at high speeds without causing undue stress on the riders. Wooden coasters are typically banked from 0 to 60 degrees. Banking track is designed to eliminate and/or reduce lateral forces such as the sensation of being tossed to the side.

The banking of the track turned out to be one of the most difficult tasks. I had to do a lot of research on Great Coaster International. I looked at several pictures of the *Wildcat* and *Roar* to get ideas of how they tracked curves and banked the track. I was on a 50 bents (vertical beams or posts of a wooden coaster) per day schedule. I built 50 bents a day, placed and tracked them in the next two days, and finished the model

---

Richmond Sound Design, Ltd manufactures hardware and software for immersive sound and show control, using MIDI and other protocols. RSD's AudioBox DSP processor both generates and spatially distributes sound effects for superior 3-D results in entertainment, retail and exhibit venues.

-Richmond Sound Design, Ltd

700 hours later, 2 weeks ahead of schedule.

Planning Stage

When modeling a coaster, you plan the construction and how things are going to happen. For example, the lower part of crossovers and bridges need to be completely finished before any structure is built over them. I plan all parts of the structure in stages according to the layers of track. Start in the middle of the structure and work out. In the case of the Gwazi project, construction logistics ate up a lot of time because there are 50+ crossovers and bridges. Some places on Gwazi had bridges over bridges.

Once you get the order of construction down to stages of bents, you can begin calculating all the material. All you really need to get your calculations is the profile and the plot plans of the roller coaster. These two prints will enable you to build the entire model.

Step One: Build a bent jig or guide. This will be one of your most important tools in making the coaster. To make a jig I use plexiglas. I draw a bent on the glass with a marker and drafting tools. This provides the right spacing for every piece of the bents. Once the entire bent is drawn on the jig, glue small pieces of plastic or wood to the jig that outline what you have drawn on the plexiglas. The pieces of the bents will lie between these jig guides. The bent leg will fit between these pieces while they are glued together. Now that you have a jig, cover it with wax paper. Super glue doesn't stick to wax paper so cut out holes in the wax paper to fit around all the pieces of plastic or wood.

Step Two: Lay the layout or plot plan on a board to the approximate scale. I normally scale my models so that 1"=10'. I used this scale with Gwazi and Great Coaster International, International Association of Amusement Parks and Attractions (IAAPA) models. Each bent is drawn on the board and numbered. If you are not working in CAD you will pull measurements from the profile plan. Now that you have the bent heights, you can start cutting the balsa wood.

Step Three: Cut strips from balsa wood panels (1/16"x3"x3' and 1/32"x3"x3')

Roller Coaster model making in progress.

and arrange them in size with a planer. You can buy a balsa wood planer in your local hobby shop for around five dollars. Cut the bent legs to the appropriate height and number each bent leg with its corresponding point on the board.

Step Four: Hold the bents together using chords, diagonal posts, and ledgers. The chords are pieces of lumber that run horizontally between the bent posts. Diagonal posts run between the chords and the ledger is the piece of lumber that the track sits on. Once you get the bents into their places, stabilize them by gluing them together with a ribbon board. Ribbon boards run horizontally to the ground and in six to nine foot intervals up to the track level.

Step Five: Now it is time to set the first stage of bents. Glue five bents in standing position and attach them together with the chords. Remember it should be in the middle of the structure and on a lower area of track.

Step Six: Batters are the next things to build. Batters are diagonal strips of wood that usually only exist on curves or high structure. They provide added support for the structure during high winds and in high-banked curves where dynamic loads exert more force than normal.

Step Seven: Laying track is next in the building stage. The track is made of strips of balsa wood that are glued to the ledges. Catwalks and handrails can be added after the track is laid. Catwalks will go on both sides of the track unless it is a high-banked turn. In high-banked turns the catwalk will go on one side of the track. Handrails go all the way around the track on the very top of the bent posts.

This is an extremely limited guide to how I build roller coaster models. Keeping to this order of operation and working through every stage of bents, it is only a matter of time before your coaster model is complete. For more information on building your own roller coaster model or to see the models I have created, visit my website at http://www.cmgmodels.com. *Chris Gray is the founder of CMG Models.*

Another great place to visit if you are interested in building roller coaster models is http://www.rollercoastermodels.com. John Hunt, the model builder of rollercoastermodels.com put together a great "build your own roller coaster model" flash demo. You must have the flash plug-in installed but it is well worth your time to get it. The demo covers how he built a model of the Riverside Cyclone. See the supplies needed to build a model and the steps involved. Hunt says to be patient when building your model, it usually takes 4 to 8 weeks. The site also offers many pictures of the various stages of model development.

Model making is not only an asset to your future as a roller coaster designer or builder, it is a valuable skill that can lead to a prominent advantage in most engineering and/or architecture programs around the country. Don't take it lightly, your future as a designer may be at stake!

Illusion Engineering provides consulting, design and production services in the disciplines of lighting, special effects and show control for themed entertainment, architectural, and exhibit/display industries. Illusion Engineering specializes in remote source illumination and display, using the latest advances in fiber optic technology.

-Illusion Engineering

G-Forces On The Human Body

Designing roller coasters is practically an art form. In the simplest terms, a designer wants to create a ride that is heart-stopping, exhilarating, thrilling, addictive, and safe. You must provide the ultimate thrill or experience but not leave the riders feeling like they have been run over by a MACK truck.

G-Forces are the various forces or pressure your body encounters on a coaster ride. Actually, negative G's is 'airtime' or coming out of your seat, while positive G's are the force your seat is exerting against you. A good design will usually not exceed 4 G's or the pressure that makes you feel as if you weigh 4 times your current body weight. Obviously, when designing a ride that descends 225 feet, as the designer, you must be sensitive to how those forces are applied to the human body. Every element of the design, from the corkscrew loops to the sudden accelerations, will put some kind of stress on the riders. Just watch the face distortions of riders shooting down the entire 225 feet of the Steel Phantom. The fate of the coaster lies in the forces and

Development, design, production, patenting of advanced entertainment technologies and systems; technology licensing; conceptual design, environmental design & ride/show development for advanced technologies; Telepresence simulations; product development/prototypes for advanced ride simulations, consumer products.

-BCAT, LLC

velocities the designer decides to apply to your body at the precise moments.

Horizontal forces as well as airtime forces also need consideration from the designer. Remember the last time you rode a coaster and how you were squashed into the corner (lateral G's) or onto the person next to you when looping around a tight corner? You felt that because when the coaster moved into the turn, your body and the coaster wanted to continue moving in a straight line. According to Ron Toomer, the designer of Kennywood's Steel Phantom, "We bank the track to push the coaster into the turn." Designers attempt to convert the momentum to downward force so you don't squish the rider next to you. However, the landscape and the space available can be limiting."

Coasters are all about gravity. The first hill is always the highest to gain enough speed to make it through the rest of the track. When the Steel Phantom opened in 1991, it was the tallest and fastest coaster ever with a 225-foot drop. "When you are building something like the Steel Phantom, you don't worry too much about making it scary. It's scary already," said Toomer. See the appendix for a list of other roller coaster designers and manufacturers.

ROLLER COASTER DESIGN SOFTWARE

So what can you do to prepare for a career in roller coaster design? Do you think you can build the world's most dangerous, gravity defying, face distorting, G-pulling thrill ride? Other than completing a degree in engineering (mechanical is a good choice), obtaining practice building models, and some experience in the industry, you can also get a feel for roller coaster design by playing simulation software such as Roller Coaster Tycoon.

Roller Coaster Tycoon allows you to design and build rides for theme and amusement parks. You can create over 50 designs from the traditional Wooden Roller Coaster to the high-tech Steel Corkscrew and the terrifying Reverse Freefall - all featuring simulated motion dynamics. You can build the greatest rides that current technology is capable of, but just like the real world, you need to stay on budget.

But it's not just about building roller coasters - you've got to look after all your guests including the less adventurous by providing the complete range of 'family' ride entertainment such as miniature railways, boat hire and mazes. Build food and drink stalls with rest facilities, hire costumed entertainers for the kids and create a park landscape that's not only fun but also appealing to walk through. Remember, you can own the best roller coaster ride ever, but if the visitors don't have a decent path to get there, your ride is a flop because success is not just a matter of building state-of-the-art rides; it's how you structure the park with themes, colors and landscaping that will help your guests enjoy the experience enough to come back and pay for more.

Playing Roller Coaster Tycoon, you answer the same questions designers of theme and amusement parks must ask themselves today such as: Why should people come to your park? Are the rides too expensive? Have you built enough food stalls? Do your amazing rides have a habit of breaking down too often? You're in charge of it all: making sure the rides are safe, finding out what your guests are thinking and giving them what they want for the right price!

An intense ride can be fun, but there's a thin line between pleasure and pain, and if your ride is too intense, you'll find that nobody will want to ride it. As a general rule, if the 'intensity' rating is over 10, the ride is probably painful rather than pleasurable, and you'll have to do some re-designing work.

Other Roller Coaster Design Resources

There are many other resources available to the aspiring roller coaster designer. Walthers Model Railroad

Mall offers Wild Mouse and Giant Dipper working roller coaster models with drive motors. These two models are very close to the real thing. The motor takes the cars to the top of the track and momentum carries the coaster through the dips and banks. See them at http://www.walthers.com.

American Coaster Enthusiasts (ACE) is a roller coaster club founded in 1978 as a not-for-profit, all volunteer club to foster and promote the conservation, appreciation, knowledge and enjoyment of the art of the classic wooden roller coaster and the contemporary steel coaster. Since 1978, ACE has grown from 3 members to over 5,000 members representing 48 states and over 20 countries. ACE publishes a magazine and newsletter for coaster enthusiasts and offers the following benefits to its members:

- Members will be able to attend all ACE events at reduced registration rates. Events typically include Exclusive Ride Time (ERT) and discounts for lodging;

- Many parks also host special events and invite members of ACE and other amusement park related clubs. Many of these events also include ERT; and

- A few parks offer free or reduced admission to ACE members.

If you want to design or are generally enthusiastic about roller coasters, you need to join the ACE. Check them out at http://www.aceonline.org.

Another important step to becoming a roller coaster designer is to realize that no matter where you live today or how old you are, you can succeed at this career. Gray said, "Never give up, I can't stress that enough. It was tough for me growing up in eastern Kentucky telling everyone that I was going to design roller coasters when I grew up. Persistence will pay off. I have made some really great friends in the amusement industry just by being persistent but not annoying. I have also been very lucky that when opportunity knocked I was there jerking it by the arm."

Ride & show engineering consultants, design rides, special effects, theater rigging, peer review of engineering designs, professional mechanical engineering services in Nevada, California and Florida. Project planning and management, dark rides, water rides, simulators, track & vehicle design. Steam train and track design.

-Hanlon Engineering, Inc.

Chapter Six

The Future Of Themed Entertainment Design

An anticipatory view of the future of themed entertainment design can be developed if we look closely at the changes we are seeing in the world today. Just 60 years ago we didn't have color television, and 25 years ago we didn't even have personal computers. Who could have predicted the power of the Internet back then. How can you predict the future 25 years from today? Technology is growing faster than ever. How can we even predict what the next 10 years will have in store for us?

If we stick to what we know about the people for whom we will design attractions, we know that we live longer, that more immigrants are coming into this country, that technology is increasing exponentially, that companies are project oriented, and there is an increased concern about security and environmental issues.

Let's look at these issues one by one.

✦   If people are living longer, you can bet that you will need to change your designs to correspond to your changing audience. Once upon a time, mom, dad, and the kids were the biggest patrons of your park. Today seniors are healthier, more lively and more wealthy. Grandma and Grandpa, retired and with more time on their hands, can take their grandchildren to theme parks or restaurants more often than mom and dad.

From a park design standpoint, this means you need to design for a wide age group. You must supply quality food, provide more educational entertainment (edutainment attractions) and attractions that show positive respectful relationships between the young and the old, provide more places to sit down and make sure you give enough sizzle for every dollar. Seniors are more discriminating, skeptical, and from living on a fixed income, they demand more quality content.

✦ As more and more people immigrate to this country, the way themed entertainment is designed will change. Your audience will diversify to include more socioeconomic classes, more ethnicities, and a wider range of perspectives. You can prepare for this ethnic change by taking language courses, increasing your amount of traveling, and taking the time to learn and become sensitive to other cultures and ways of life.

✦ The capabilities of technology are increasing exponentially. "More lights, more sounds, more intensity and more experience" is the motto of the up and coming generation. Technology's impact on people must accommodate our dwindling attention spans. Attractions must be faster, more entertaining, become more meaningful, be more theatrical, provide more variety and be more intense than ever before.

Ten years ago people were satisfied with the corkscrew type of roller coaster. Today we have rides like Superman the Escape: a 30 second ride that goes straight up 41 stories, has 9 seconds of zero gravity, then plunges backwards the 41 stories at 100 miles per hour.

As an entertainment designer, how will you top that?

✦   We have all seen the growing trend of downsizing as companies focus on their core activities. To stay competitive, management teams are advised to run lean and mean. Waste is eliminated as well as redundant efforts. The entertainment industry is no exception. Many companies hire contractors or temporary staff on a project-by-project basis to keep their overhead costs as low as possible. Even the contractors are hiring contractors. See the appendix of this book for a listing of some of the companies you can work for that the giants such as Disney and Universal Studios hire as contractors.

✦   On December 31, 1999 when the clock was about to bring in the new year, there was a tense moment as people wondered if terrorists

It's Alive Co. is an independent consulting firm dedicated to providing the best in Show Technical Management Consulting. Including project management, technical direction, and creative consulting for themed environments and attractions globally including themed retail and restaurants, theme parks, museums, casinos, and visitor centers.

-It's Alive Co.

had infiltrated a highly populated area such a Walt Disney World. Security is a very important issue in themed attraction design. If your guests do not feel safe, they will not frequent your establishment. Ways you can design for safety include the standard blow-out walls already in place in locker rental areas, eliminating dark or hidden hallways, and by designing attractions that promote well-being rather than violence. Mortal Combat type action video games are great for home entertainment, but the effects of being submerged in a themed world of shooting, fighting, and violence may not be good for your patrons. Your environment should be relaxing, reduce tension and promote fun for all.

EMPLOYMENT OUTLOOK

"Developing a theme park is typically a large-scale multimillion dollar project and the engineers involved go through periods of 'feast or famine'

> RLH Enterprises specializes in providing mechanical and projected special effects for themed environments of all kinds, including theme parks, destination resorts, museums and expositions. Services span the entire project life cycle starting from concept development and proceeding through design, engineering, production, installation, and maintaince. RLH Enterprises has provided special effects for projects worldwide.
>
> -RLH Enterprises LLC

depending on who's building a park at the time. Their work is mission critical and very specialized," said Jim Presnal, Executive Director of the Themed Entertainment Association.

According to Maris Ensing of Mad Systems, "There are some people who work for a company and some that work free-lance. A lot of work is not on-site, but in the office. On average, 50/50 is more likely for someone who spends a lot of time on site. Ordinary technicians may end up doing a bit more (i.e., people like electricians who are putting cables in), but project managers do less. For us, most of the work is done in the office/lab: designing the system, procuring things, testing, building racks, testing the final system, etc. Then we ship it out to the job site. To give you an example, two of the jobs we're currently doing will take a month in the office/lab on and off, and then about 3-4 days on site."

"As time passes, it's become more and more difficult to have people who are NOT on staff, quite simply because anyone working for you for more than a certain percentage of their time cannot be a consultant (U.S. government regulations) which means that a lot of people have to be hired. The salary range varies enormously - some people get more than they can get elsewhere because of luck or because they have particular skills, and some don't because a lot of these jobs are in high demand. They are a lot more interesting than most. The majority of people I know in the industry tend to stay in it rather than move into something else (i.e., more boring)."

When you work on contract an important thing to remember is that although the initial pay may be excellent or significantly more than a non-contract job, you will receive no benefits or retirement and when the project is over, you will lose your job. Taking benefits and retirement into account, your salary will be comparable to non-contract engineers in other industries.

MUSEUMS AND SCIENCE CENTERS

Museums and Science centers going multimedia/ edutainment are the wave of the future. Public funding for these institutions is being spread thinner and thinner every year. As more people in our nation begin to retire (remember they are living longer too), the funds available through social security will begin to

---

Entech provides engineering, design and fabrication services to the amusement, entertainment, museum, casino, and retail industries. We specialize in show action attractions, custom ride and track systems, animatronics and mechanical, hydraulic and pneumatic technology to provide special effects. Entech's division, Orlando OnSite Services, offers support to out of town vendors needing shop services or materials during their installation process. "We engineer and fabricate fun."
-Entech Creative Industries

dwindle and the current funding received by the arts will also be less. As a result, museums and science centers will be funded by corporations, taxpayers, grants, and donations.

This can be good news if you enjoy state-of-the-art science museums like the Tech Museum of Innovation in San Jose, CA, in the heart of the Silicon

State of the art robotic praying mantis in lifelike environment at Sci-Port Discovery Museum in Shreveport, Louisiana.

Valley. Evidence of this funding switch is already prevalent in the high tech science centers springing up all over the United States. According to Gillian Thomas, Chief Executive of Bristol 2000, "People throughout the country have seen it as an occasion to make a difference. An opportunity to look at what we are doing, to challenge the current thinking and look for new ways forward. For once, money is available to back the ideas and realize the dreams."

The upside for entertainment designers is more venues for employment. The challenge lies in bringing high quality entertainment under the umbrella of an enthusiastic, inspirational, and promotional form of education. This is no easy task. "Educators have become aware that an understanding of science may not rub off on visitors when they play with exhibits quite as easily as everyone had hoped," said Gillian. How will you reach them?

VIRTUAL REALITY EXPLODES

Virtual Reality (VR) is a hot new technology that promises a bright and prosperous future for the entertainment industry. More and more interactive applications primarily in entertainment are emerging through VR. The computer-generated imagery is getting more realistic, and the lag time, once a significant problem, has been reduced largely due to technological advances such as increasing processor speeds.

VR can be used to build the models and/or simulations we talked about in chapter one. A virtual model can also save on time and model fabrication costs. A virtual model can allow customers to walk-through a work in process before any construction has taken place.

Feature Article - Virtual Reality (Bytes)
by Beth Sherry

Virtual reality (VR) may already be at a mall near you-in games where players control battle simulators, explore distant planets, dodge dinosaurs, and play virtual sports like racquetball, tennis, and golf. The Vivid Group in Toronto, Canada, developed a VR game called FutureSport, and in one volleyball match, opponents from Canada and Italy played simultaneously, with the game data transmitted from computer to computer by satellite.

Using a sensor-lined glove, joystick, or mouse and special headset, VR users can visit, move around in, and touch objects that exist only in computer-generated worlds. Images surrounding the viewer are seen in 3-D through view screens built into the headset. The core of every VR application is a high-power computer database that builds and displays graphic images, senses the user's head and body movements, and adjusts what the user sees. But, VR has applications far beyond the latest arcade game.

The National Aeronautics and Space Administration (NASA) and the Department of Defense developed the first VR systems for flight simulation. Space crews training at Johnson Space Center in Houston use a virtual reality system programmed with the physics of orbit. Astronauts take virtual space walks and are able to practice making repairs to their crafts before attempting them in space.

Biomedical engineers are using virtual reality techniques to help surgeons reconstruct facial birth defects. Engineers and physicists at General Electric's Corporate Research and Development Center convert

---

Providing comprehensive design integration & production management services. They are instrumental in the staging of Broadway, corporate meetings and events for Fortune 500 Corporations and themed attractions such as the Rio's Masquerade in the Sky Show and Niketown, New York. Entolo is a division of the Production Resource Group.

-Entolo

hundreds of CT scans into digital information that's programmed to produce near photographic 3-D reproductions of a patient's head - both inside and outside. This allows surgeons to use an "electronic scalpel" to explore nerves and underlying structures prior to performing reconstructive surgery.

VPL Research, Inc., in Redwood City, California, with assistance from NASA, developed the DataGlove, a microprocessor-based Lycra glove that converts hand gestures and positions into data that's transmitted from the glove to the host computer. Greenleaf Medical Systems of Palo Alto, California, has used the glove to determine how much the different joints of a human hand can bend, and they are developing technologies that allow doctors to accurately measure hand injuries.

Superior is a full service staffing organization providing qualified temporary and direct professionals to the themed entertainment industry in the following areas: theme park development, architecture, engineering, project management, show production, set design, creative design, graphics, writing, special effects, model shop, audio/ visual, skilled craftsman, information technology and administrative support.

- Superior Technical Resources

Architectural firms are using the technology to design "virtual offices" and homes to improve traffic flow, design more efficient layouts, and create open spaces. Home owners, wearing VR helmets and gloves, can design living spaces, lay out furniture, and customize their kitchens, reaching out to open cabinets and deciding where to place appliances. When they are satisfied, the computer will draft detailed drawings for the actual job. Recognizing the influence of computers on architecture, Massachusetts Institute of Technology began a three-year, multimillion dollar program to rebuild its design studio.

Many European companies, including Rolls Royce, Vickers Shipbuilding and Engineering, and ICI Chemicals and Polymers have pooled their engineering talents to form the Virtual Reality and Simulation initiative

---

Interesting Products designs, manufactures, and installs liquid nitrogen (LN2) effects equipment and systems for entertainment and architectural applications. Dry Fogger® and Fog Stick™ products create ground fog, fog curtains, clouds, and LN2 burst effects in manual and automated control environments. Fog Diverters™ and Curtain Manifolds™ distribute fog to multiple points for a variety of effects applications. Design services are available.

- Interesting Products

to apply computer simulation and visualization to industrial design and 3-D modeling projects. Virtual reality provides a window into other worlds. We are only just beginning to discover what's on the other side of the looking glass. *Extracted from Engineering Today's and Tomorrow's Entertainment by Beth G. Shery of the American Institute of Chemical Engineers.*

Another up and coming application of VR is VR Theme Parks. In 1990, a park called Virtual World opened in Chicago. Players are in individual cockpits or pods in this location-based entertainment system. Players choose between two games and play against up to eight other players.

An example of a future virtual theme park is Final Jvstice©. For the first time in history, a blockbuster movie premiere will coincide with the launch of an amusement park boasting the same name and theme. An amusement park theme is usually marketed as an afterthought once the film that inspired it has made its gross in the box office. But in the case of Final Jvstice©, the movie experience is merely a glimpse into a high-tech playground. While the top-budget sci-fi epic, Final Jvstice©, crowds theatres nation wide, the same set used to film this special effects masterpiece will be open to the public. Guests will be allowed to roam freely throughout the set in the form of a fully-immersive, fully-interactive amusement park experience!

When the park opens, there will be a cast of over 300 actors and actresses playing the roles of the unusual alien species that will bring life to the attraction. The aliens may be too busy shuffling about to notice that the guests are even there!

To satisfy the nerves of the avid thrillseeker, Final Jvstice© the Theme Park boasts a fully-interactive ride experience that combines state-of-the-art looping steel roller coaster technology, motion simulation, a video game, and a movie ride—all in one! The ride, simply called Final Jvstice©, is the hallmark of the entire experience. Final Jvstice© dares to do what no other thrill ride has ever dreamed—it will allow the rider to actually control the level of intensity at any time during the ride!

Final Jvstice© seamlessly blends roller coaster thrills with visual effects that seem to surround the riders in all directions. Special effects will be combined in such a way that riders will have no clue where reality ends and the virtual world begins. Amplified speakers behind the seats will help immerse the rider's senses by pumping over 200 watts of sound effects and music through their bodies! Watch for it!

As technology pulls the world in different directions and changes the way we think about entertainment, designers must be flexible to the changing expectations of their audience.

Chapter Seven

What Do I Do Now?

Theme park design is a fascinating blend of creativity, ingenuity and technical expertise. The people involved in entertainment are highly motivated and deadline oriented. If you want to get into this industry begin now! Contact a few of the companies listed in the appendix and pursue an internship or co-op possibilities. Contact TAC Entertainment Staffing and get your foot in the door by working as a mechanic, or controls technician for the first two years. Observe the industry from the inside, decide where you would like to work and the best way to get hired.

According to Bob Chambers, the Managing Director of It's Alive Co., "The observation I have made about our industry is that the most productive engineers in the business started out working for several fabrication vendors before working directly for the big park owners. These vendors are, in reality, the life blood of the industry, because the park owners come up with the creative ideas (most of time not using much engineering input) and end up hiring the fabrication vendors to design and build the individual effects, rides, etc."

As a themed entertainment designer, remember that you will be working in teams in almost every phase of ride and show development. Communication and patience are essential. Upper management may not have a good understanding of engineering principles, and you may not have a good understanding of the marketing or promotional aspects of your design. "Engineers are only one piece of the complex interaction required to complete the project with minimum cost, minimum schedule, and maximum guest impact," said Chambers.

Theme parks are evolving. As an aspiring designer you may wonder if they will have an impact on the culture of tomorrow. The parks of today focus primarily on make-believe worlds, but if the audience is getting older, will there be a desire for a park of days gone by such as a nostalgia park? Perhaps parks can have family values or diversity themed attractions. Women may enjoy attending a Woman's World theme park and couples can rekindle relationships in a lover's paradise.

We can use theme parks to visit foreign countries or learn about a region's culture. Splendid China, a theme park in Kissimmee, Florida, is already bringing the Far East to the United States. This park has a half-mile replica of the Great Wall and a four-story high Buddha. Another park, Old Tucson Studios, is a western theme park that brings the culture of the old west to the many visitors of the United States. Waimea Falls Park, a Hawaiian paradise theme park, educates visitors on the islands culture. You can enjoy breath-taking cliff-diving, learn about the healing medicinal herbs, tour the "House of Bones" burial site, find you have a talent for o'o'ihe (spear throwing), or discover fishing secrets at Hale Wa'a (canoe house).

Parks can also be constructed for special interest groups such as sports enthusiasts or churches. Perhaps VR can be combined to completely immerse the customer in the special interest group environment. Imagine making the winning touchdown in the Superbowl or attending church in another country.

With the economy booming, the opportunities for themed entertainment designers are on the rise. Hard work, sound training in the fundamentals of engineering design and the ability to apply those fundamentals will exponentially increase your chances of landing your dream job. All of the contributors to this book have advised (in some way or other) that you prepare yourself using the tips previously mentioned, respect the work, persevere, and above all, have fun!

Recommended Reading
Industry Magazines

Amusement Business Online
Web: www.amusementbusiness.com

Amusement Today Magazine
Tel: (817) 460-7220
Web: www.amusementtoday.com

Attractions Management Magazine
Tel: +44 (0) 1462 431385
Web: www.attractions.co.uk

Cinefex Magazine
Tel: (909) 781-1917
Web: www.cinefex.com

Entertainment Management Magazine
Tel: (203) 790-9330
Web: www.entertainment-centers.com

E-Ticket Magazine
Web: www.the-e-ticket.com

Funworld Magazine (included with an IAAPA membership)
Tel: (703) 836-4800
Web: www.iaapa.org/products/pub-adop.htm

Graduating Engineer and Computer Careers Magazine
Tel: (609) 243-9111
Web: www.graduatingengineer.com

Haunted Attraction Magazine
Tel: (843) 626-2369
Web: www.hauntedamerica.com

InterPark Magazine
Tel: +44 (0)161 633 0100
Web: www.interpark.co.uk

Midway Museum Publications
Tel: (603) 883-9405

Park World Magazine
Tel: +44 (0)161 624 3687
Web: www.datateam.co.uk/business.htm

Sound & Video Contractor Magazine
Tel: (800) 441-0294
Web: www.svconline.com

Tourist Attractions & Parks Magazine
Tel: 610-734-2420
Web: www.aimsintl.org

Althoff Dave, Jr., "The Roller Coaster Almanac" 1999

Basta, Nicholas, *Opportunities in Engineering Careers*, VGM Career Horizons: 1990.

Belcher, M. Clay, "What is Architectural Engineering?" University of Kansas: 1993.

Bolles, Richard Nelson, *What Color is your Parachute?: A Practical Manual for Job Hunters and Career Changers*, Ten Speed Press: 1993.

"Careers in Science and Engineering: A Student Guide to Grad School and Beyond," National Academy Press:1996.

Etzkowitz, Henry, Carol Kemelgor, and Michael Neuschatz, "Barriers to Women in Academic Science and Engineering," John Hopkins University Press: 1994.

Ferrell, Tom, "Workplace 2000: Engineering," Peterson's Job Opportunities for Engineering and Computer Science Majors 1998.

Gabelman, Irving , "The New Engineer's Guide to Career Growth and Professional Awareness," IEEE Press: 1996.

"The Green Report: Engineering Education for a Changing World," American Society for Engineering Education: 1998.

Imagineers, The, *Walt Disney Imagineering: A Behind the Dreams Look at Making the Magic Real*, Hyperion: 1996.

Landis, Raymond, "Enhancing Student Success: A Five Step Process for Getting Students to 'Study Smart'," American Society for Engineering Education: 1998.

Landis, Raymond, "Enhancing Engineering Student Success: A Pedagogy for Changing Behaviors,": 1997.

Landis, Raymond B., *Studying Engineering: A Roadmap to a Rewarding Career,* Discovery Press: 1995.

LeBold, William K. and Dona J. LeBold, "Women Engineers: A Historical Perspective," American Society for Engineering Education: 1998.

Love, Sydney F., *Planning and Creating Successful Engineered Designs: Managing the Design Process*, Advanced Professional Development Incorporated: 1986.

Mogel, Leonard, *Careers in Communications and Entertainment*, Simon & Schuster: 2000.

Morgan, Robert P., Proctor P. Reid, and Wm, A. Wulf, "The Changing Nature of Engineering," ASEE PRISM. May-June 1998.

Nekuda, Jennifer, *Structural Engineering*, University of Kansas: 1997.

Peterson, George D. "Engineering Criteria 2000: A Bold New Change Agent," American Society for Engineering Education: 1998.

Reynolds, Robert R., *Roller Coasters, Flumes and Flying Saucers: The Story of Ed Morgan and Karl Bacon Ride Inventors of the Modern Amusement Parks*, Northern Lights Publishing: 1999.

Schafer, Mike and Rutherford, Scott, *Roller Coasters: Enthusiast Color Series*, MBI Publishing Company: 1998.

Sheeter, Kim, *Guide to North America's Theme Parks*, American Automobile Association: 1997.

Sherwood, Kaitlin, "Women in the Engineering Industry," Society of Women Engineers at UIUC lecture: 1994.

"Simple Machines", Society of Women Engineers Career Guidance Module: 1996.

"Student Science Training Programs for Precollege Students," Science Service, Inc.: 1994.

Tieger, Paul and Barbara Barron-Tieger, *Do What You Are: Discover the Perfect Career for You through the Secrets of Personality Type*, Little, Brown and Company: 1995.

"Today's News and Views for Tomorrow's Engineers," *The ASME Mechanical Advantage:* 1997.

Vanderheiden, Gregg, "Thirty Something (Million): Should They Be Exceptions?" Trace Research and Development Center, Waisman Center and Department of Industrial Engineering, University of Wisconsin-Madison:1996.

Zibart, Eve, *The Unofficial Disney Companion: The Inside Story of Walt Disney World and the Man Behind the Mouse*, Macmillan Travel: 1997.

Trade Associations

The Amusement Industry Manufacturers and Suppliers,
International
Tel: (941)953-3101
Web: www.aimsintl.org

IAA-Interactive Amusement-Ride Association
Tel: (800) 572-0523
Web: www.aimsintl.org/iaa.htm

IAAPA - International Association of Amusement Parks &
Attractions
Tel: (703) 836-4800
Web: www.iaapa.org

IAFEC - International Association of Family Entertainment
Centers
Tel: (603) 464-6498
Web: www.iafec.org

NAARSO - National Association of Amusement Ride
Tel: (800) 669-9053
Web: www.naarso.com

OABA - Outdoor Amusement Business
Tel: (800) 517-OABA
Web: www.oaba.org

The Themed Entertainment Association
Tel: (818) 843-8497
Web: www.teaonline.org

World Waterpark Association
Tel: (913) 599-0300
Web: www.waterparks.com

Appendix

Employment Resource Directory

THEMED ENTERTAINMENT COMPANIES

The following company directory lists some of the entertainment companies that hire engineers. This appendix is not comprehensive and is only meant to be a guide to aid your search for your dream job. If you are interested in a specific employer please call or write the organization listed for the most current information available.

1220 Exhibits
7550 Exchange Drive
Orlando, FL 32809 : USA
Tel: (800) 390-1220
Fax: (407) 855-2206
Email: dhughes@1220.com
Web: www.1220.com
Employment Contact: General Manager

Anitech Systems, Inc.
25021 Anza Drive
Valencia, CA 91355 : USA
Tel: (661) 257-2184
Fax: (661) 257-2025
Email: steve@anitech-systems.com
Web: www.anitech-systems.com

Arthesia
Rosenthalerstr. 46/47
Berlin , D-10178 : Germany
Tel: (49) 30 284 68 0
Fax: (49) 30 284 68 222
Email: arthesia@arthesia.com
Web: www.arthesia.com

Attraction Services
28145 Avenue Crocker
Valencia, CA 91355 : USA
Tel: (661) 257-2802
Fax: (661) 257-2810
Email: Mtownsend@asblt.com
Web: www.AttractionServices.com

AVG, Inc.
9144 Deering Avenue
Chatsworth, CA 91311 : USA
Tel: (818) 998-0100
Fax: (818) 998-0233
Email: Mail@a-v-g-com
Web: www.a-v-g.com
Employment Contact: Exec. VP

BCAT, LLC
10560 Dolcedo Way
Los Angeles, CA 90077 : USA
Tel: (310) 472-4766
Fax: (310) 472-2977
Email: bcat@pacbell.net
Web: bcat.org

Canton Consulting Group
P. O. Box 18886
Encino, CA 91416 : USA
Tel: (818) 981-6842
Fax: (818) 705-7606
Email: jcanton@compuserve.com
Employment Contact: John E. Canton-Owner

Entech Creative Industries
9603 Satellite Blvd. Suite 150
Orlando, FL 32837 :USA
Tel: (407) 251-9898
Fax: (407) 251-9904
Email: gallagher@EntechCreative.com
Web: www.EntechCreative.com
Employment Contact: Director of Sales

Entolo
539 Temple Hill Rd.
New Windsor, NY 12553 : USA
Tel: (914) 567-5752
Fax: (914) 567-5800
Web: www.prg.com
Employment Contact: Human Resources

Edwards Technologies, Inc.
139 Maryland St.
El Segundo, CA 90245 : USA
Tel: (310) 536-7070

Fax: (310) 322-1459
Email: briane@edwardstech.net
Web: www.edwardstech.net
Employment Contact: VP of Operations

Frank Weigand & Associates
P. O. Box 5332
Glendale, CA 91221-5332 : USA
Tel: (818) 957-5135
Fax: (818) 957-6296
Email: fkWEIGAND@aol.com
Employment Contact: Frank Weigand-Principal

Gallegos Lighting Design
8132 Andasol Avenue
Northridge, CA 91325 : USA
Tel: (818) 343-5762
Fax: (818) 343-2041
Email: gldla@gallegoslighting.com
Web: www.gallegoslighting.com
Employment Contact: Patrick Gallegos-Principal

Garner Holt Productions, Inc.
825 E. Cooley Avenue
San Bernardino, CA 92408 : USA
Tel: (909) 799-3030
Fax: (909) 799-7351
Email: info@garnerholt.com
Web: www.garnerholt.com

Gary E. Thompson, Television Engineering Services
P. O. Box 27476
Los Angeles, CA 90027 : USA
Tel: (323) 665-0019
Fax: (323) 662-3067
Email: Gthompson1@compuserve.com
Employment Contact: Gary E. Thompson-Owner

Hanlon Engineering, Inc.
3185-F2 Airway Ave
Costa Mesa, CA 92626 : USA
Tel: (714) 641-4094
Fax: (714) 641-4091
Email: hei@prodigy.net
Web: http://www.hanloninc.com
Employment Contact: Mark Hanlon-VP Engineering

Harmonix Music Systems, Inc.
675 Massachusetts Ave
Cambridge, MA 02139 : USA
Tel: (617) 491-6144
Fax: (617) 491-7411
Email: kathleen@harmonixmusic.com
Web: www.harmonixmusic.com
Employment Contact: VP of Engineering

Harvest Moon Studio
3534-A Larga Ave.
Los Angeles, CA 90039 : USA
Tel: (323) 668-2000
Fax: (323) 668-2011
Email: info@harvestmoonstudio.com
Web: www.harvestmoonstudio.com

Holmes & Narver
999 Town & Country Road
Orange, CA 92668 : USA
Tel: (714) 567-22400
Fax: (714) 567-2767
Email: worthy@hninc.com
Web: hninc.com

Industrial Light and Magic (ILM)
P.O. Box 2459
San Rafael, CA 94912 : USA
Job Hotline: (415) 258-2100
Web: www.ilm.com
Employment Contact: Human Resources

Illusion Engineering
12541 Amboy Avenue
Sylmar, CA 91342-3604 : USA
Tel: (818) 367-7442
Fax: (818) 367-7322
Email: PAMulder@aol.com
Web: www.illusion-engineering.com
Employment Contact: Paul Mulder-Owner

Interesting Products, Inc.
806 N. Peoria St.
Chicago, IL 60622 : USA
Tel: (312) 738-5220
Fax: (312) 738-3330

Email: ln2fog@attglobal.net
Web: www.interesting-products.com
Employment Contact: Larry Schoeneman-President

International Aquatic Consultants
3226 W. Desert Inn. Rd.
Las Vegas, NV 89102 : USA
Tel: 702-368-4100
Fax: 702-368-6247
Email: cmillburn@intlaquatic.com
Web: www.intlaquatic.com
Employment Contact: VP Engineering

ITEC Entertainment Corp., Inc.
8544 Commodity Circle
Orlando, FL 32819 : USA
Tel: (407) 226-0200
Fax: (407) 226-0201
Email: opportunities@itec.com
Web: www.itec.com
Employment Contact: HR Manager

It's Alive Co.
4110 Rincon Avenue
Montrose, CA 91020 : USA
Tel: (818) 248-0876
Fax: (818) 248-1796
Email: Bob_Chambers@ItsAliveCo.com
Web: www.ItsAliveCo.com
Employment Contact: Human Resources Department

Lazarus Lighting Design, Inc.
4131 Vanowen Place
Burbank, CA 91505-1311 : USA
Tel: (818) 956-3211
Fax: (818) 956-3233
Email: LLDINC@aol.com
Web: www.lldinc.com
Employment Contact: Brett Jay Lazarus-President

Leisure & Recreation Concepts/LARC, Inc.
2151 Fort Worth Avenue
Dallas, TX 75211-1899 : USA
Tel: (214) 942-4474
Fax: (214) 941-5157
Email: larc@airmail.net

Web: www.larcinc.com
Employment Contact: Michael A. Jenkins-President

Lucci & Associates
3251 Corte Malpaso Suite 511
Camarillo, CA 93012 : USA
Tel: (805) 389-6520
Fax: (805) 389-6519
Email: cadd@lucciland.com
Web: lucciland.com
Employment Contact: Ken Lucci-President

M B & A Consulting Mechanical Engineers
115 S. Lamer St.
Burbank, CA 91506 : USA
Tel: (818) 845-1585
Fax: (818) 845-6433
Email: MBA115@aol.com
Employment Contact: Mel Bilow-Principal

Mad Systems
15415 Redhill Ave. Ste B
Tustin, CA 92780
Tel: (714) 259-9000
Fax: (714) 259-9001
Email: madsystems@home.com
Web: www.madsystems.org

MediaMation, Inc.
2461 W. 205th St. B100
Torrance, CA 90501 : USA
Tel: (310) 320-0696
Fax: (310) 320-0699
Email: mediamat@aol.com
Web: www.mediamat.com
Employment Contact: Dan Jamele-President

Nassal Company, The
415 W. Kaley St.
Orlando, FL 32806 : USA
Tel: (407) 648-0400
Fax: (407) 648-0841
Email: jbinder@nassal.com
Web: www.nassal.com
Employment Contact: Operations Manager

Oceaneering Entertainment Systems
501 Prince Georges Blvd.
Upper Marlboro, MD 20774 : USA
Tel: (301) 249-3300
Fax: (301) 390-1305
Email: dwelch@adtech1.oceaneering.com
Web: www.oceaneering.com
Employment Contact: Manager

Parsons Infrastructure and Technology
100 W. Walnut St.
Pasadena, CA 91124 : USA
Tel: (626) 440-2293
Fax: (626) 440-2702
Email: michael.brady@parsons.com
Web: www.parsons.com
Employment Contact: VP Entertainment

Penwal Industries, Inc.
10611 Acacia Street
Rancho Cucamonga, CA 91730 : USA
Tel: (909) 466-1555
Fax: (909) 466-1565
Email: staff@penwal.com
Web: www.penwal.com
Employment Contact: Human Resources Manager

Pixar Animation Studios
1001 West Cutting Blvd.
Richmond, CA 94804 : USA
Tel: (510) 236-4000
Fax: (510) 236-0388
Job Hotline: (510) 412-6017
Web: www.pixar.com
Employment Contact: Recruiting Manager

Production Arts Lighting
7777 Westside Ave.
North Bergen, NJ 07047: USA
Tel: (201) 958-4000
Fax: (201) 868-7249
Web: www.prg.com
Employment Contact: Steve Terry-President

Projex International
9555 Hierba Road
Agua Dulce, CA 91350-4564 : USA
Tel: (661) 268-0999
Fax: (661) 268-1885
Email: 71570.457@compuserve.com
Web: www.projexinternational.com
Employment Contact: Richard Graham-President

R H Productions
142 W. 36th Street 16th floor
New York, NY 10018 : USA
Tel: (212) 967-6040
Fax: (212) 967-6113
Email: Rhproductions@rhproductions.com
Employment Contact: Robin Reardon-President

Rando Productions, Inc.
1829 Dana Street
Glendale, CA 91201 : USA
Tel: (818) 552-2900
Fax: (818) 552-2388
Email: rpiefx@rpiefx.com
Web: www.rpiefx.com
Employment Contact: Joe Rando

Richmond Sound Design, Ltd.
205-11780 River Road
Richmond, BC V6X 1Z7 : Canada
Tel: (604) 718-0860
Fax: (604) 718-0863
Email: charlier@show-control.com
Web: http://www.show-control.com
Employment Contact: Charlie Richmond-President

Scenery West
11461 Hart St.
North Hollywood, CA 91605 : USA
Tel: (818) 765-8661
Fax: (818) 765-5495
Email: sceneryw@earthlink.net
Web: www.scenerywest.com
Employment Contact: Human Resources Dept

Scharff Weisberg, Inc.
599 Eleventh Avenue
New York, NY 10036 : USA
Tel: (212) 582-2345
Fax: (212) 757-6367
Email: swinyc.com
Web: www.swinyc.com
Employment Contact: Office Manager

Setpoint Engineered Systems, Inc.
2835 South Commerce Way
Ogden, UT 84401 : USA
Tel: (801) 621-4117
Fax: (801) 621-4165
Email: setpoint@setpointusa.com
Web: www.setpointusa.com
Employment Contact: HR Director

Show Fountains, Inc.
P. O. Box 8522
The Woodlands, TX 77387 : USA
Tel: (281) 288-3500
Fax: (281) 288-3538
Email: info@showfountains.com
Web: www.showfountains.com
Employment Contact: Michael Connery-President

Sigma Design Group
1507 Ashland Avenue
Santa Monica, CA 90405 : USA
Tel: (310) 452-2292
Fax: (310) 452-4073
Email: sigmagn@aol.com
Web: www.sigmadesigngroup.com
Employment Contact: Gerald Nash-President

Solutions for Engineering & Business
6634 Valmont St.
Tujunga, CA 91042-2561 : USA
Tel: (818) 951-1999
Fax: (818) 951-5919
Email: dtoyne@itcom.net
Web: solutionsfor.com
Employment Contact: David Toyne - President

Superior Technical Resources
21221 S. Western Ave. Suite 110
Los Angeles, CA 90501 : USA
Tel: (310) 781-3004
Fax: (310) 781-3013
Email: hodgesp@superior-sdc.com
Web: www.superior-sdc.com
Employment Contact: Branch Manager

TAC Entertainment Staffing
3500 W. Olive Ave. Suite 660
Burbank, CA 91505
Tel: (800) 766-9050
Fax: (818) 557-0870
Web: www.tacentertainment.com or www.ShowBizJobs.com

Tilden Lobnitz Cooper
1717 S. Orange Ave. Suite 300
Orlando, FL 32806 : USA
Tel: (407) 841-9050
Fax: (407) 425-7367
Email: pwm@tlc-engineers.com
Web: www.tlc-engineers.com
Employment Contact: HR Director

Universal Studios Strategic Staffing
P.O. Box 8152
Universal City, CA 91618-8152

Walt Disney Imagineering
1401 Flower St.
P.O. Box 25020
Glendale, CA 91221-5020
Tel: (818) 544-6500
Employment Contact: Walt Disney Imagineering Human Resources

Walt Disney - MGM Studios
Feature Animation
P.O. Box 10,000
Lake Buena Vista, FL 32830

ROLLER COASTER DESIGNERS AND MANUFACTURERS

Antonio Zamperla s.p.a.
36077 Altavilla Vicentia (Italy)
Via Monte Grappa, 15
Tel: 390-444-573133
Fax: 390-444-573720
49 Fanny Rd (USA)
Parsippany, NJ 07054-0598
Tel: (973) 334-8133
Fax: (973) 334-6880
Email: zamperla@zamperla.it
Web: www.zamperlarides.com

Arrow Dynamics, Inc.
P.O. Box 160038
Clearfield, UT 84016-0038
Tel: (801) 825-1611
Fax: (801) 776-2671
Web: www.arrowdynamics.com
Employment Contact: Human Resourcs

Birket Engineering
PO Box 610190
Ocoee, FL 34761
Tel: (407) 290-2000
Fax: (407) 654-2150
Email: Staffing@birket.com
Web: www.birket.com
Employment Contact: Staffing

Bolliger & Mabillard Consulting Engineers, Inc. (B&M)
Chemin des Dailles 31
Monthey, 1870
Switzerland
Tel: 41-244-721580
Fax: 41-244-719584

Chance Rides
4219 Irving
Wichita, KS 67209
Tel: (316) 942-7411
Fax: (316) 942-7416
Email: jobs@rides.com
Web: www.rides.com
Employment Contact: Human Resources Manager

Costasur, Inc.
6311 Wiehe Rd.
Cincinnati, OH 45237-4213
Tel: (513) 731-5225

Custom Coasters International, Inc. (CCI)
8461 Cinti-Columbus Road
West Chester, OH 45069
Tel: (513) 755-0626
Fax: (513) 777-2658

Great Coasters East
RR #3 Box 148-A
Sunbury, Pennsylvania 17801
Tel: (570) 286-9330

Great Coaster West
P.O. Box 4033
Santa Cruz, CA 95083
Tel: (831) 464-9551
Fax: (831) 464-8967
Web: www.greatcoasters.com

Intamin AG
Verenastrasse 37
Wollerau, 8832
Switzerland
Tel: 41-178-69111
Fax: 41-178-50202
Email: info@intaminworldwide.com
Web: www.intaminworldwide.com

Intamin Ltd.
8258 Veterans Hwy., Suite 2
Millersville, MD 21108-1457
Tel: (410) 987-5404
Fax: (410) 987-5078

John Pierce & Associates/Roller Coaster Corporation of America (RCCA)
P.O. Box 888506
Atlanta, GA 30356-0506
Tel: (770) 448-7931
Fax: (770) 263-0176

Miler Coaster Co., Inc./International Coaster, Inc.
P.O. Box 20548
Portland, OR 97294-0548
Tel: (503) 256-3019
Fax: (503) 255-2153

Miller and Baker/D.H. Morgan Manufacturing
450 McQuaide Drive
La Selva Beach, CA 95076-1921
Tel: (831) 724-8686
Fax: (831) 724-7882
Web: www.dhmorgan.com
Employment Contact: Human Resources

O.D. Hopkins Associates, Inc.
40 Park Lane
Contoocook, NH 03229
Tel: (603) 746-4131
Fax: (603) 746-3659

Overland Amusement Company/Philadelphia Toboggan Coasters, Inc. (PTC)
Eighth & Maple Streets
Lansdale, PA 19446-1848
Tel: (215) 362-4700
Fax: (215) 368-9680

Premier Rides, Inc.
401 Headquarters Dr.
Millersville, Maryland 21108
Tel: (410) 923-0414
Fax: (410) 923-357?
Email: xtremrides@aol.com
Web: www.premier-rides.com

Reverchon Manufacturing USA
6460 Sargasso Way
Jupiter, FL 33458
Tel: (561) 741-4644
Fax: (561) 741-4645
Email: reverchonpp@cs.com
Web: www.reverchon.com

Rides & Parks International
P.O. Box 6361
Arlington, TX 76005-6361

Tel: (972) 660-3322
Fax: (972) 660-0620
Email: info@zierer.com
Web: www.zierer.com

Roller Coaster Corporation of Texas/TOGO International, Inc.
100 Merchant St., Suite 150
Cincinnati, OH 45246-3751
Tel: (513) 772-8408
Fax: (513) 772-8601
Web: www.rcca.com

S&S Power
350 West 2500 North
Logan, UT 84341
Tel: (435) 752-1987
Fax: (435) 752-1948
Web: www.s-spower.com

Vekoma/Showquest Entertainment (The Netherlands)
P.O. Box 8006
Posterholt, 6060 AA
The Netherlands
Tel: 31-475-409222
Fax: 31-475-402115
Web: www.showquest.com

Index